英漢對照韻譯

毛澤東詩詞

辜正坤 譯注

March, 2002.

To Mr. & Ms.
Doug and Amy Sonheim

Gu Zhengkun

北京大學出版社

北京

圖書在版編目（CIP）數據

毛澤東詩詞：英漢對照韻譯/毛澤東著；辜正坤譯注。
北京：北京大學出版社，1993. 10
  ISBN 7-301-02313-8

Ⅰ. 毛…
Ⅱ. ①毛…②辜…
Ⅲ. ①毛主席詩詞-注釋 ②毛主席詩詞-對照讀物-英、漢
Ⅳ. A44

出版者地址：北京大學校內　郵政編碼：100871
排　印　者：北京大學印刷廠
發　行　者：北京大學出版社
經　銷　者：新華書店
850×1168 毫米　32 開本　11 印張　265 千字
1993 年 10 月第一版　1998 年 7 月第四次印刷
定　　價：18.00 圓

POEMS OF MAO ZEDONG

with rhymed versions and annotations

Translated and annotated

by

Gu Zhengkun

Peking University Press

Beijing, China, 1993

This book includes 45 poems by Mao Zedong, with rhymed English versions and lucid, matter-of-fact annotations. The translation is superbly done, faithful to the original in content, beautiful in form and diction; the annotations are detailed and instructive, enlightening the reader with regard to allusions, themes and general background of Mao's poetry. The book is thus praised as a version of rare quality ever produced both at home and abroad. Morever, a long introduction is given, offering a general survey of Mao's poetry with regard to its ideological content, artistic style, imageries, language and so on. Three letters of Mao discussing poetry are provided in the Appendices, helping the reader gain an insight into Mao's aesthetic view of poetry. In addition, the original, as a contrast to the English version, is printed in the traditional complex form of Chinese characters along with their phonetic symbols.

目　録

CONTENTS

正　編

6

副　編

Part Two

FOREWORD

The poet whom we are to read occupies a curious but assured position in the history of 20th century Chinese literature: curious, because he was one who theoretically advocated with all his heart the development of modern poetry —— the free verse written in the vernacular —— and even hopefully asserted that the bright future of Chinese poetry lay right in the development of folk-songs, yet in practice, he himself never wrote poetry in plain Chinese but in a completely traditional and classical style; assured, because he composed the poetry so well that, at his best, few modern Chinese poets can rival him. To western minds, he is a political giant who, though shaking old China to its foundation, remains a debatable figure as to his contribution to the creation of a better world. But what captures our attention here is Mao the poet, not Mao the statesman; still politically a subject of controversy at home and abroad, he is, however, almost universally acknowledged as a successful poet of rare talent, even, to a moderate degree, by his sworn enemies.

Needless to say, when we approach this man called Mao Zedong (1893—1976), we will not forget he was the leader of the People's Republic of China, a country teeming with the largest population in the world, as well as a son of a peasant family in Shaoshan, Hunan Province. True, as a poet he wrote in a tradition of thousands of years from the ages of *The Book of Odes* through

Qu Yuan (340 B. C. -278 B. C.),Li Po (Li Bai,701—762),Du Fu (Tu Fu,712—770)to Su Dongpo (Su Shi,1037—1101). He did, however, distinguish himself from his predecessors; and what particularly marks him out as a celebrated poet is, as many believe, his enormous breadth of mind, unbounded aspiration and his dauntless daring, which often go beyond the commonly conceived poetic universe. And this alone, I make bold to say, is justification enough to rank Mao among the poets of the first order.

Remember, too, the fact that he was not one of those professional lyrical singers who spend all their lives improving their art, but a fighter as well as a military commander charging and storming fortresses, composing a few lines here and there between life and death. Each piece finished is believed to be a window into his personality, an insight into his whole being, a mouthpiece of his spirit and soul.

To do him justice, as a poet playing upon a traditional lyre, he sings occassionally out of the classical tune, but on the whole, his rhymes sound so pleasant to the ear that during the Cultural Revolution the whole China echoed his songs with a frantic enthusiasm so that he was more quoted than any other poet in any other country in any other age. The great impact of Mao's poetry upon the contemporary Chinese culture, particularly, contemporary Chinese literature, is strongly felt everywhere in the east. And this, as you may agree, justifies rendering Mao's poetic efforts into a foreign language.

To say Mao's poetry is characterized by an enormous breadth of mind and an unbounded aspiration does not mean Mao writes with pure high-sounding slogans; instead, Mao seems deliberately to avoid revealing his ambitions in a straightforeward way. Often, he favours the technique that puts landscape and human emotion side by side so that the landscape becomes the exponent of his aspirations. Here are lines from his much-quoted "Snow" that surely make the reader spellbound and serve to exemplify my point:

A thousand li of the earth is ice-clad aground
Ten thousand li of the sky is snow-bound.
Behold! At both sides of the Great Wall
An expanse of whiteness conquers all;
In the Yellow River, up and down,
The surging waves are gone!
Like silver snakes the mountains dance,
Like wax elephants the highlands bounce,
All try to be higher than heaven even once!

Never before has modern Chinese literature had a poet whose description of landscape can rival that of Mao in breadth and power! The endless earth, the unbounded sky, the longest wall, the largest river, the dancing mountains, and boundless highlands, all are submerged in an expanse of whiteness——snow and ice, and meanwhile, all come alive through the strokes of Mao's painting brush, for it is a picture both poetically existing in the eye of poet's mind and realistically seen "on this small globe": realities and illusions overlap and merge themselves, thus one cannot tell whether it is the grand scene that comes in the eye of poet's mind, or the mind that gives birth to the grand scene. If we know that in Chinese "rivers and mountains" usually is a metonymy for political power, we understand what Mao here drives at: "All try to be higher than heaven even once": a possible allusion to cruel strifes for state power on the part of so-called "heroes".

Of course, the poet is not content with just giving a majestic description of the spatial view, further, his mind's eye penetrates through the heavy curtain of time into history gaping for the ambitious adventurers:

> With so much beauty is the land endowed,
> So many heroes thus in homage bowed.
> The first king of Qin and the seventh king of Han,
> Neither was a true literary man;
> The first king of Song and the second king of Tang,
> Neither was noted for poetry or song.
> Even the Proud Son of Heaven, for a time,
> Called Genghis Khan, in his prime,
> Knowing only shooting eagles over his tent
> With a bow so bent.

All those emperors and kings so illustrious and renowned once in history are only worthy of a casual mention; according to Mao's standard, they are not "truly great men".

Thousands of li of space and thousands of years of time thus criss-cross under Mao's pen like a network of meridians and parallels. The poem begins with the majestic sweep of heaven and earth, yet ends with a note of regret:

> Alas, all no longer remain!
> For truly great men,

One should look within this age's ken.

To draw a conclusion from the ending lines that Mao entertains an imperial ambition is obviously at odds with Mao's own explanation that "truly great men refer to the proletariat" (see note 8 to the poem in the text), i. e. a group of great men, not only one. The point here is —— I hope the assertion will not be wide of the mark —— that Mao himself never refused to claim to belong in the group. He deserves the name, and more.

A similar note rings familiar in many of Mao's other poems such as "To Yang Kaihui" where the poet is believed to attempt a revolution in the south of China:

> *Just as Mount Kunlun suddenly topples down,*
> *Or the typhoon sweeps the world adown.*

or as "Changsha" where the young scholar, standing "in the autumn chill", "under the frosty and vaulted sky", "with feelings and thoughts evoked to" his tongue,

> *cannot help asking the land so immensely wide and long*
> *Who can hold up or sink you down?*
> *......*
>
> *We were young as schoolmates,*
> *All in our prime without taints,*
> *Imbued with young scholars' daring,*
> *We defied all restraints.*
> *We criticised the state affairs then,*
> *With vigorous strokes of the pen,*
> *To us, nothing but dung were those big men!*

or as "March from Tingzhou to Changsha"where the commander
trumpets a call:

> To uproot the corrupt and evil in June
> God sends armies strong
> To bind roc and whale with a cord
> of ten thousand feet long.

or as "Jinggang Mountain" where Mao hails proudly:

> Only, our sentiments and aspirations so high
> Are like the bright moon hanging in the distant sky,
> Like the wind and thunder majestically sweeping by.

or as "Mount Liupan" where the poet chants aloud:

> High on the peak of Mount Liupan,
> In the west wind red flags flap and sound.
> We now hold the long cord in hand,
> When will the Dragon be bound?

or as "Seeing Jūu Ichro off to Japan" in which Mao brings his fel-
low men to attention:

> Take care of the cultivation
>   of your body and mind, and do
> Keep the sun and moon
>   in your heart beautiful and new.
> Just five hundred years past
>   since the birth of the last great man,
> All the other figures in power now
>   are of a mediocre clan.

These lines were written early in 1918 alluding to Mencius'
well-quoted prophesy:"There must appear a great king every five
hundred years."(See the part ii of the chapter"Gong Sunchou"in
The Book of Mencius.)It is thought inappropriate to call Mao a
great king,but it is agreed in the communist world as proper and
fitting to call him a great man. The greatness of such a great man
must accordingly characterize his poetry, thus the breadth of
mind,the great aspiration and the daring in spirit become almost
necessary attributes to the poetry of Mao Zedong,as if to confirm
old Buffon's dictum:"The style is the man himself."

But it may do Mao Zedong injustice to think that his poetry
is merely characterized by boldness,breadth of mind,or high aspirations. The bulk of his poetry that amounts to about 50 pieces
does include those sounding in different notes;some are romantically tender,or even sentimental enough to coax us into tears.
Read his"To Yang Kaihui" and you find how young lovers can be
deeply attached to each other and how they can be heartbroken
bearing an inevitable separation:

> *Hands waving from you off I start,*
> *How can I bear to see you*
> *face me with an aching heart.*
> *Retelling me your sorrows as we part.*
> *Grief is written over*
> *your brows and in your eyes;*
> *You wink back the hot tears*
> *about to break ties.*
> ......
> *In this world only you and I*

7

in each other's hearts dwell;
For how can heaven tell
If man suffers hell?
......
With a sound of the whistle
our hearts break and moan,
Henceforth I embark on a journey
to the world's end alone.

So this man of herculean build was not always a fighter with a heart of stone but also one' in whose soul burnt an inner-most longing for true love and tenderness. This persistent love-longing stuck to the poet so strongly that even 34 years later in 1957 in a poem entitled "Reply to Li Shuyi, to the tune of Butterflies Love Flowers", Mao still passionately lamented the loss of his wife Yang Kaihui, the proud Poplar:

You lost your darling Willow and I my Poplar proud,
Both Poplar and Willow soar gracefully above the
cloud.

Perhaps it needs to be poinetd out that what differentiates Mao from other poets in treating the love theme is Mao's efforts to avoid an utter indulgence in love's illusions bordering on senti-mentality. Often, his songs end in a spirited tone or merry mood that helps both the author and the reader exert themselves for loftier aspirations; thus in "Reply to Li Shuyi" we read

The lonely goddess of the moon spreads her sleeves long,
To console the loyal souls she dances in the sky with a
song.

> *Suddenly the news about the tiger subdued comes from*
> *the earth,*
> *At once the rain pours down from our darling's tears of*
> *mirth.*

Similarly in "To Yang Kaihui", the poet does not allow himself to be a slave to sadness of separation for long; the ending couplet again echoes the author's usual militant spirit.

Sometimes, Mao tends to invest his lines with a touch of philosophical meditation. For instance, in "The Immortal's Cave", Mao concludes that

> *The unmatched beauty dwells on the lofty and perilous peak.*

This seems to suggest that superb victory must be accompanied by a lot of hardships and setbacks and that God prefers to put the best things where people do not frequent. In "The People's Liberation Army Captures Nanking", Mao declares, not without a note of pride, that "The change of seas into lands is man's world's true way."

In "Reading History", one of the masterpieces in Mao's collection of poetry, we are deeply impressed by Mao's genuine concern for man's destiny and by his view of man's history:

> *In the human world it is hard to find a grinning smile;*
> *Killing his own brethren was man's practice vile.*
> *Alas, the land so fair*
> *Is soaked in blood everywhere.*

The lament is soul-shaking; the mankind's history is one of suffering, blood and death. The fair land is put in sharp contrast to the ugly side of human nature：men have kept slaughtering each other for thousands of years.

Comparatively speaking，there are not so many classical allusions in Mao's poetry as in the outpourings of the most traditional singers. But Mao surely never deliberately avoids using them; whenever he feels it necessary he always makes use of them properly and successfully. For example，in "Against the First 'Encirclement' Campaign"，Mao gives a note to the proper name"Mount Buzhou"in which a legendary figure"Gong Gong" is referred to as a hero who can even turn the heaven and the earth upside down. A careful reader might notice that in Chinese "Gong" in the name"Gong Gong" and the "Gong" in the name "Gong Chan Dang"(the Communist Party)are the same both in spelling and pronunciation，thus he can easily relish Mao's pun：Gong Gong in the 24th - 23th century B. C.. is compared to"Gong Chan Dang"(the Communist Party of China)in the 20th century，A. D.. Another example is the use of the historical figure Xiang Yu(232 B. C. — 202 B. C.)in the poem"The People's Liberation Army Captures Nanking"："Ape not King Xiang for a fame of mercy in a lucky hour". Xiang Yu was a leader of nobles of the Qin Dynasty，who，like Liu Bang，was later a rebel leader rising in arms against the Qin Dynasty. After the downfall of the Qin Dynasty，Xiang Yu was supposed to be the strongest of the rebel leaders，yet，for a name of playing fair with one's opponent，Xiang Yu gave up two chances to kill Liu Bang. And，as foreseen by Xiang Bo，Xiang Yu's military advisor，Liu Bang later on，by going back on his promise，staged a surprise attack upon Xiang Yu and finally destroyed his powerful troops. With Mao，the allusion

10

is related to a suggestion made by some people at home and abroad that the Chinese Communist Party could come to terms with the Kuomintang government before the People's Liberation Army crossed the Yangzi River on condition that C. P. C. be the master of the land north of the Yangzi River while K. M. T. be the ruler of the land south of the River. Mao refuses such suggestions by adroitly employing the allusion above which clearly visualizes his viewpoint more convincing than any other long article: Chiang Kai-shek is Liu Bang and C. P. C. is not going to be Xiang Yu or to be destroyed by a possible breach of the peace treaty on the part of K. M. T.. Allusions of the kind are many in Mao's poetry; a close examination of them will bring to light what lies beneath the surface of the poetic diction. This sort of examination has been made in translator's notes to each poem.

To appreciate Mao's poetry, one needs to know something about Mao's aesthetic view of the poetic creation. In a letter to Chen Yi, Mao firmly maintains that poetry conveys ideas through images (See Appendices "A Letter to Chen Yi about Poetry"). And in practice, Mao's reliance on concrete imagery is evident; this can be further attested by his extensive use of rhetorical figures such as similes, metaphors, personification and metonymy. One of the most distinguishing features of Mao's poetry that Chinese scholars have so far failed to point out, is that, Mao never put into his traditional-styled poems such words as Soviet Revisionism, U. S. Imperialism, feudalism, bourgeoisie, Marxism, Leninism, the Communist Party, Japanese invaders, which, as is often the case, appear in most works of the other communist writers or poets, with a frequency so high as to dampen the reader's enthusiasm for relishing a literary work. Literature, after all, is an art, speaking in the form of emotion, imagery or plot, not merely in a set of concepts or terms. As a poet, Mao did know his line, much better than many Chinese contemporary poets, say, Guo Moruo, who has been frowned upon by some readers for using too many slogans and technical terms in his tradtional-styled poems, highly vernacular as well as undisguisedly flattering. It does not mean that Mao's poetry is immune to political propaganda; on the contrary, many scholars clearly perceive that each piece penned by Mao in the collection is highly political. One should remember Mao's noted essay "Talks at the Yenan Forum on Literature and Art" (May 1942) in which Mao asserts that literature and art are bound to, and must, serve politics. Mao's poetry is the very exponent of his own literary theory; the point is that in poetic wording Mao tends to poetize politics rather than politicalize poetry, at least on the surface. Thus we experience a strange or unique literary phenomena, i. e. Mao's highly political poetry does not sound political at all while some so-called love poems by modern Chinese poets often read like political demagogy or moral sermons. A foreign reader may, at a glance, feel puzzled over some recurring words in Mao's poems like "thunder and storm", "red", "dragon", which often, though not always, symbolize revolution, the Red Army forces, Chiang Kai-shek, etc., respectively. Take "Winter Clouds" for example, where "winter clouds" stands for the grim political situation in 1962 for C. P. C; "flowers" for Marxist parties in the world; "cold waves" for the revisionist trend of thought; "warm breeze" for the gradual rising of the Marxist organizations and parties; "heroes" for the proletariate headed by the communist parties; "leopards and tigers"for imperialists; "wild bears"for Soviet revisionists; "plum blossoms" for true Marxist parties and organizations, or in particular, the Chinese Communist Party; and "flies" for sham Marxists, opportunists, traitors and so on. Thus it is reasonable for the reader to think that, without the knowledge of this sort of background information, one's understanding of Mao's poetry is bound to incur a danger of being vague and discursive. But the logic could be a bit flexible. As we have mentioned before, Mao's poetry, though usually highly political, is never a mechanically didactic sermon; instead, it is often astonishingly original and beautiful in form and expression, i. e. always conveying ideas through concrete images. And images, as is known, can evoke aesthetic associations of many kinds; and each aesthetic judgement, in my opinion, is valuable to the reader. Therefore, a western reader can, on one hand, ignore all that concerns political background, and take for granted Mao's poetry, or in other words, take them at face value, simply as a close text of pure poetic creation independent of the author; he might as well calmly receive whatever comes to mind when he first bumps into those pieces, enamoured of their beautiful images, words, phrases, ideas, themes or sounds, paying no attention to the author's original implication, allusions or so on. On the other hand, the same western reader, if he pleases , can also try to grasp Mao's poetry at a cultural, political, or economic level by looking into the translator's notes which provide necessary background information. Certain images, words or phrases that frequently occur in Mao's poems may call for detailed studies on the part of the expert. Here are

13

some examples. Of about 50 poems by Mao, 30 poems include 40 places that refer to mountains. This is surely not an accidental phenomenon; the frequency, rather, is an evidence of Mao's affinity with mountains, and also is an revelation and expression of Mao's background as a peasant son whose childhood was spent in his native place Shaoshan where mountains were a daily sight, and as an army commander whose traces covered the greater part of the mountainous districts of China. No wonder Mao Zedong the strategist who most vehemently upheld the strategy of "encircle the cities from the rural areas and then capture them" seldom described cities or towns in fairly concise and visionary images as he did mountains in manifold and varied shapes and colours. Statistics show Mao's poems are mostly written with reference to Hunan, its scenery, its cultural tradition, its natives and so on. The fact may be explained by an artistic demand that a successful poet must write about what he feels most familiar with; that Muses sing better in their own native tongues. A view that is prevalent among Chinese literary circles is that Mao's poetry is vivid, concrete and an exact representation of Mao Zedong Thought. In a sense, it stands to reason. However, I feel like to remind the reader of the version of the fact that Mao is here presented first of all as a poet, not as a philosopher, a military commander, a political leader, nor as a scholar or moral didact. He surely played all the roles, but as author of a collection of poetry, he should be done justice by being treated mainly as a poet, or we fall into the romantic convention that criticism of poetry often completely relapses into criticism of the character and way of life of the poet, so far as these would be inferred from his outputs.

We read him chiefly to appreciate the beautiful, the feeling of the agreeable, the inherently pleasant, not a set of moral rules or philosophical doctrines which, if we like, can be acquired by persuing his prose works.

Many others insist that Mao's poetry embodies the whole process of the Chinese proletarian revolution. Of this I venture to voice a different opinion. Since the poetry was written in different periods and arranged in an anthological order, it certainly reflects some aspects of the Chinese social changes during a period of about 50 years, but to say it reflects the whole process of the Chinese proletarian revolution is insignificant and inappropriate as far as the historical truth is concerned. Insignificant, because Mao was not writing a history of the Chinese revolution composed of detailed facts but writing poetry mainly aiming to give himself and others aesthetic pleasure or serve to boost the people's morale; his lyrical production, therefore, no matter how minute in its description, can only fragmentarily record some historical happenings which do not chiefly exist for the sake of history itself but rather for the sake of poetry; as far as the precision, bulk and objectivity are concerned, compared with the historical facts recorded in those formal history books of the Chinese revolution, the detailed descriptions provided by the poems, after all, are insignificant; inappropriate, because some impotant historical phases are missing in the poems, e. g. the War of Resistance against Japan waged in China for eight years has not been mentioned even once! So the poems are far from being a complete record of the whole process of the modern Chinese revolution. The point is, Mao's poetry can be of epic element, but is not necessarily intended or explained as a history of any social changes.

For years, interpretations of Mao Zedong's poetry had been offered in a somewhat exaggerated mode. Critics or scholars in the field tended to focus on what was called the political purport. Mao was described as a Jesus-like saint who had only the salvation of human beings in mind yet never thought of tender feelings such as love or fatherly affection. He was supposed to be bent on using poetry as a powerful weapon to expound Mao Zedong Thought, to conquer enemies, to criticise what he called imperialism, revisionism and reactionaries. But today, as his contemporaries, we know through our common sense that he was never a superman nor a god but an ordinary man living among us sharing with us his poetic outpourings. We understand him not because of his extraordinariness but because of his very ordinariness. Or in other words, we understand Mao the man not through his images of earth-shaking heroism but through these harmonious and overpowering numbers now gathered here in this collection.

All translation must unavoidably involve an act of interpretation. The principle that guides my interpretation is "never adhering to only one single principle". Poetry, in its essence, defies monistical understanding and explanation. Very often, interpretations are multiple as well as valuable though not of the same validity. A wise interpreter is inclined to be open-minded to any artistic product, because any interpretation can be right when judged from different angles. Thus pluralistic points of view are usually preferred when I observe an aesthetic object. In a broad sense, every one of us is a qualified appraiser of poetry. It may be pleasant for the 20th century reader to muse on the fact that beauty in modernized society is no longer the priviledged luxury favouring only what was called great artists, poets, connoisseurs and aesthetists; rather, it is liberated from the grip of the beauty-monopolist, say, from the trap of Hegel's aesthetic system. Now any work of art can, on one hand, be subject to criticism from the professional aesthetic critics or theorists, and, on the other, more often be evaluated, appreciated or condemned by the reader's response. The old attempt to be the authority of interpretation of literary works seems to be scorned as an illusion. Human culture in its entirety today faces up to an inevitable trend of decentralization. All this may sound true. But, when modernists or postmodernists are busy with revolting against the past, they are making more grave mistakes than their predecessors ever made in the past, because they do not understand if man exists, he instinctively needs a focus for his existence; if man wants to progress, he needs a point of departure so that he is able to start. That starting-point internally as well as externally moulds his way of future action; he has to be one-sided, one-dimensional. Or in other words, man has to choose. The key point here I want to make is that man should make choices yet without prejudice against the other possibilities. It is the same case with my interpretation of Mao Zedong's poetry. On one hand, I deem all the explanations valuable; on the other, I more often stick to one. I respect all, but I have my choice. Thus the reader will find in translator's notes some points are given more than one explanation listed as 1), 2), 3)... etc., but in more cases, a single explanation is given.

Juggling with the often conflicting goals of literalness and literacy, fidelity and felicity, can never be done to everyone's satisfaction. Traditionally speaking, Mao's poems in this collection have all been composed in fairly strict rhyme patterns which, to the understanding of any one who knows more or less about classic Chinese poetry, contribute much not only to the musicality of poetry but also sometimes to the conception of original ideas or imagery, for, as J. Peletier remarks "la contrainte de la rime favorise l'invention et la création" (H. Weber, *La Création Poétique au 16e Siécle en France*, I, 155); or as Xie Zhen (1495—1575), a noted poet and poetic theorist in the Ming Dynasty, says, "rhymes can invite poetic ideas" and "a single rhymed word sometimes generates a whole line. " (*The Complete Works of Siming Shanren*, Vol. 22, Chapter 24). What with the need for an implication that Mao's poetry is rhymed and what with the consideration as above, a rhymed version of Mao's poetry is naturally required though other sorts of versions, say, versions without rhyme, are certainly also needed to further a combined effort of rendering Mao's work into English in its totality of both artistic forms and ideological connotation. Thus in doing the translation, I have been cautiously on tiptoes—— not because of Mao's importance of being head of more than one thousand million Chinese people but because of his being a unique poet like others deserving an equal treatment on the part of the translator—— to retain the original word order and spareness of diction while still producing a reasonably fluent and rhymed English version allowing it to stand, as much as possible, on its own.

　　The earliest poem written by Mao can be traced back to 1918, and during the following 47 years, Mao Zedong as one can expect, must have written many poems, but until now only a small percentage of them has seen publication. Generally speaking, Mao's poems are grouped into Part One and Part Two. Part One includes 42 poems which were all revised by Mao himself and were formally published in newspapers, journals or selections of Mao's poetry in different periods of time when Mao was still alive. Part Two includes 7 poems which appeared in various publications in recent years without the author's approval and revision; some of them were once explicitly mentioned by Mao as unsatisfactory and he bluntly refused to publish them either for the sake of political consideration or for the sake of artistic blemish. However, they have now become so current in many Chinese publications that their absence in the present edition of the English version would be a great pity especially for those English-speaking readers who wish to read Mao's poetry in its entirety. Fortunately, the quite manageable size of Mao's corpus —— approximately 50 poems, makes it comparatively easy for a translator and annotator to gain an insight into the sum of his poetic world. But in China, the poetry of Mao Zedong has been the subject of extensive critical studies in literary circles ever since the publication of the first selection of Mao's poems (18 in all) in 1957. Controversies over many points were so perplexing and intricate that occasionally Mao Zedong himself had to be invited to offer certain explanations. The translator and annotator has set great store by these explanations which, whenever possible, have been carefully quoted in the translator's notes. However, in doing so, the annotator also keeps in mind that poetry writing and poetry appreciation are not always the same thing; it often happens that a poet does not understand his own production better than someone else. Thus taking for granted Mao's every word about his poetry is not sagacious, the case being more so when certain special factors such as Mao's unique position and other subsequent political subtleties are taken into account. And this also implies that no matter how hard and carefully the translator and annotator may try to tackle his job, he can never expect his attempt to be one of perfection; thus he feels only too ready to bow to any criticism from any scholars, experts and readers in general.

Another thing worth mentioning is that, for the sake of convenience of foreign readers, all the English versions of Mao's poetry have been given their Chinese originals with Chinese phonetic symbols. Moreover, the original Chinese characters have all been printed in their complex forms rather than in their simplified equivalents. This arrangement is made in the belief that the original Chinese complex characters, being pictographs (hieroglyphs) to a considerable extent, can conjure up in our minds more picturesque associations, thus more condusive to conceiving poetic associations than simplified characters. But, of course, this does not mean that the author thinks of the complex form as being superior to the simplified one in a general sense. Every value has its particular usage: the simplified form, for instance, is as good or better than the complex one as far as its merit of being written easily is concerned.

Again, the arrangement of the Chinese characters and their phonetic symbols is unconventional either. The editor in charge of the book, maintains that the reason phonetic symbols have not been placed right under each of the characters is chiefly based on a consideration that too much space between the characters might damage their aesthetic effect while the present design serves to retain the original flavour of the conventional Chinese character arrangement; after all, phonetic symbols are only auxiliary to the Chinese characters. Perhaps, at the first glance, readers might find it strange, but they will soon get used to it and learn which phonetic symbol is for which character.

Last but not least, completing a book of this magnitude requires not only the sustained engagement of the translator and annotator, but also the guidance, encouragement, support and criticism from various people whom I should like to acknowledge with heartfelt gratitude. My thanks first go to Professor Li Funing of Department of English, Peking University, for his brilliant guidance and studied perusal of my manuscripts; to Professor Fredric Jameson of Duke University of the United States, for his cordial encouragement; to Professor Xu Yuanzhong of Peking University for his valuable idea of how to render a version of classical Chinese poetry beautiful in thought, sound and form; to Professor Luo Jingguo of Department of English, Peking University, for his intelligent advice on certain poetic treatment; to Mr. George Whiteman, the well-known owner of Shakespeare &. Company, Paris, for his clever polishing of my work; to Mr. Morgan Godwin, editor and writer, Paris, for his witty comment on my foreword; to Professor Claude Fischer of Oxford University of Great Britain for his constructive opinion of my first draft; to Professor Jonathan Turner of UNESCO (Paris) for his timely help in providing me with his private store of necessary books. Thanks also go to Professor Hu Shuangbao, the editor in charge of the book, for his competence and great efforts in bringing the volume to fruition; to David Porter, doctoral candidate of Stanford University of the United States for his kind help and suggestions; finally, to Zhao Hong, my wife, doctoral candidate of Peking University, for her good counsel and laborious proofreading of the whole book.

UNESCO Paris, France   *Gu Zhengkun*
April, 1993

一九九三年四月於法國巴黎
聯合國教科文總部

正　编

Part One

賀 新 郎

hè xīn láng

揮手從茲去。

huī shǒu cóng zī qù

更那堪凄然相向，

gèng nà kān qī rán xiāng xiàng

苦情重訴。

kǔ qíng chóng sù

眼角眉梢都似恨，

yǎn jiǎo méi shāo dōu sì hèn

熱淚欲零還住。

rè lèi yù líng huán zhù

知誤會前番書語。

zhī wù huì qián fān shū yǔ

過眼滔滔雲共霧，

guò yǎn tāo tāo yún gòng wù

算人間知己吾和汝。

suàn rén jiān zhī jǐ wú hé rǔ

人有病，

rén yǒu bìng

TO YANG KAIHUI[1]
to the tune of Congratulating Bridegroom

Hands waving from you off I start[2].
How can I bear to see you
    face me with an aching heart,
Retelling me your sorrows as we part.
Grief is written over
    your brows and in your eyes,
You wink back the hot tears
    about to break ties.
I know, you misunderstood
    my former letter to you,
But like clouds and mist
    the misreading soon away flew,
In this world only you and I
    in each other's hearts dwell.
For how can heaven tell
If man[3] suffers hell?

天知否？

tiān zhī fǒu

今朝霜重東門路，

jīn zhāo shuāng zhòng dōng mén lù

照橫塘半天殘月，

zhào héng táng bàn tiān cán yuè

凄清如許。

qī qīng rú xǔ

汽笛一聲腸已斷，

qì dí yī shēng cháng yǐ duàn

從此天涯孤旅。

cóng cǐ tiān yá gū lǚ

憑割斷愁絲恨縷。

píng gē duàn chóu sī hèn lǚ

要似昆侖崩絶壁，

yào sì kūn lún bēng jué bì

又恰像颱風掃環宇。

yòu qià xiàng tái fēng sǎo huán yǔ

重比翼，

chóng bǐ yì

和雲翥。

hé yún zhù

（一九二三年）

This morning on the road to the East Gate[4]
    heavy frost is seen to lie,
The waning moon over the Pond[5]
    lingers half way down the sky,
So sad and clear on high.
With a sound of the whistle[6]
    our hearts break and moan,
Then I set out on a journey
    to the world's end alone,
And thus cut off in brief
The string of sadness and grief
Just as Mount Kunlun's cliffs
    suddenly topple down,
Or the typhoon sweeps the world adown.[7]
    Then in a pair we will soar
    Into the clouds once more.

(1923)[8]

TRANSLATOR'S NOTES

1. Yang Kaihui: born in 1901, a native of Changsha, Hunan Province. She got married with Mao Zedong in 1920 and joined the Communist Party of China in 1921. In October, 1930, she was arrested by the Kuomintang authority in Changsha and killed on November 24 of that year.

    This poem was first published in the *People's Daily* (September 9, 1979).

2. Hands waving from you off I start: In April, 1923, Zhao Hengti, the warlord of Hunan Province, issued an order to arrest Mao Zedong; Mao thus left Changsha for Shanghai. In the summer of that year, Yang Kaihui, too, arrived in Shanghai for a reunion with Mao; they stayed there engaging themselves in revolutionary activities for a short time and then together came back to Changsha in the autumn. Possibly in October or November of the same year (the definite time now remains unclear), Mao Zedong went to Guangzhou alone to help Sun Yat-sen with the preparation of the First National Congress of Kuomintang. This line is just a reference to Mao's second separation from Yang Kaihui at Changsha.

3. man: a pun possibly implying 1) the poet himself; 2) individuals in general; 3) the Chinese people living in hot waters at that time. Some critics tend to think the last implication is more acceptable than the other two, for it echoes lines 17-18 where the poet is believed to attempt a revolution in the south of China.

6

4. the East Gate:also called Xiaowumen,a side gate in the east of the city of Changsha.

5. the Pond:referring to Clear Water Pool(Qingshuitang)outside the East Gate where Mao Zedong and Yang Kaihui lived from 1921 to 1923.

6. the whistle:the whistle of the train the poet got on. There was a railway station near the Pond.

7. Just as ... the world adown:These two lines are believed by some scholars to hint at a great revolution to come in the south of China.

8. 1923:In June of that year,the Third National Congress of the Communist Party of China was held in Guangzhou,Guangdong Province. Mao Zedong was present at the meeting and elected executive member of the Central Committee of C. P. C. The Congress adopted "Proposals on National Movements and Kuomintang", intending to build up a revolutionary united front in cooperation with K. M. T. under the leadership of Sun Yat-sen.

沁園春
qìn yuán chūn

長　沙
cháng shā

獨立寒秋，
dú lì hán qiū

湘江北去，
xiāng jiāng běi qù

橘子洲頭。
jú zǐ zhōu tóu

看萬山紅遍，
kàn wàn shān hóng biàn

層林盡染；
céng lín jìn rǎn

漫江碧透，
màn jiāng bì tòu

百舸爭流。
bǎi gě zhēng liú

鷹擊長空，
yīng jī cháng kōng

CHANGSHA[1]

*to the tune of Spring beaming
in Garden*

At the head of the Orange Island[2]
Alone I stand in the autumn chill,
Watching the Xiang[3] flow north still.
Lo ! Ten thousand mountains[4] are clothed
    in red[5]
With serried maples all dyed through,
And the river so purely blue,
While ships try racing ahead.
Eagles soar undauntedly on high,
Fish hover in the limpid deep,
For freedom all creatures with each other
    vie,
Under the frosty and vaulted sky. [6]
With feelings and thoughts evoked to my
    tongue,
I cannot help asking the land so immensely

魚翔淺底，
yú xiáng qiǎn dǐ

萬類霜天競自由。
wàn lèi shuāng tiān jìng zì yóu

悵寥廓，
chàng liáo kuò

問蒼茫大地，
wèn cāng máng dà dì

誰主沉浮？
shuí zhǔ chén fú

携來百侶曾遊。
xié lái bǎi lǚ céng yóu

憶往昔崢嶸歲月稠。
yì wǎng xī zhēng róng suì yuè chóu

恰同學少年，
qià tóng xué shào nián

風華正茂；
fēng huá zhèng mào

書生意氣，
shū shēng yì qì

揮斥方遒。
huī chì fāng qiú

指點江山，
zhǐ diǎn jiāng shān

wide and long:
Who can hold you up or sink you down?

Here with many of my friends I often came,
And memories of arduous years now remain
    the same.
We were young as schoolmates,
All in our prime without taints,
Imbued with young scholars' daring,
We defied all restraints.
We criticised the state affairs then,
With vigorous strokes of the pen,[8]
To us, nothing but dung were those big
    men![9]
Ah, remember, do you,
While swimming in the midstream, we sent
    up waves
That stayed even the flying canoe?[10]

(1925)

11

激揚文字，
jī yáng wén zì

糞土當年萬戶侯。
fèn tǔ dāng nián wàn hù hóu

曾記否，
céng jì fǒu

到中流擊水，
dào zhōng liú jī shuǐ

浪遏飛舟？
làng è fēi zhōu

(一九二五年)

TRANSLATOR'S NOTES

1. Changsha: the provincial capital of Hunan Province. Mao Zedong came to Changsha in 1911 when he was eighteen years old. There from 1913 to 1918, he studied in No. 1 Normal School of Hunan Province. At the near end of that period with the joint efforts of He Shuheng, Cai Hesen, Chen Cang, Zhang Kundi, Luo Xuezan and others, Mao Zedong sponsored and organized New People Society aiming to transform China into one of new system. During the May Fourth Movement, the Society developed into an organization of seventy-eight members. In 1919, Mao Zedong taught in Changsha, meanwhile, editing the journal *Xiang River Review* (*Xiangjiang Pinglun*) in which he published many articles advocating revolutionary ideas. In September, 1920, still in Changsha, and again with He Shuheng and others, he set up the Communist Group of Hunan. It was not until 1923 that he left Changsha for Shanghai for the first time. In autumn, 1925, when he went to Guangzhou, he passed by Changsha where he revisited the Orange Island and Yuelu Mountains. The poem records the experiences of his last visit to Changsha.

   This poem was first published in *Poetry* (January, 1957).

2. the Orange Island: an islet in the Xiang River west of Changsha, noted for its delicious oranges.

3. the Xiang: the longest river in Hunan, originating in Guangxi, flowing by Changsha and northward to the Dongting Lake.

4. Ten thousand mountains: many mountains, here specifically referring to Yuelu Mountains southwest of the Changsha city.

5. clothed in red: Yuelu Mountains are covered with maple trees which, under the attack of autumn frost, usually become red.

6. the frosty ... sky: implying deep autumn.

7. Who can hold you up or sink you down: who can control the rise and fall of the country's destiny.

8. Imbued with ... vigorous strokes of the pen: See note 1. Mao Zedong was the organizer as well as the leader of many revolutionary activities then in Changsha. For instance, in September, 1915, Yuan Shikai intended to preclaim himself emperor, Mao Zedong wrote and distributed a pamphlet against Yuan's evil intention, though Tang Xiangming, a warlord of Hunan, severely forbade any anti-Yuan activities. In 1919, there broke out a movement to drive away Zhang Jingyao, a warlord of Hunan; again, Mao was one of the leaders of the movement.

9. big men: referring to warlords in general as well as warlords in particular such as Tang Xiangming, Fu Liangzuo and Zhang Jingyao who were warlords of Hunan.

10. swimming in the midstream ..., the flying canoe: Mao Zedong was a good swimmer ever since his childhood. Zhou Shizhao, one of Mao's middle school classmates thus recalled in an article entitled "The Roar of the Xiang River": "At midautumn night, about ten of them went by a small rowboat to the midstream of the Xiang River for viewing and admiring the full moon ... the small rowboat loaded with their songs, laugh-

14

ters and high aspirations moved around the ten-mile-long Orange Island. They came back very late; all was silent. " (See *New Newspaper of Hunan*, December 28, 1962.)

菩薩蠻
pú sà mán

黄 鶴 樓
huáng hè lóu

茫茫九派流中國，
máng máng jiǔ pài liú zhōng guó

沉沉一綫穿南北。
chén chén yī xiàn chuān nán běi

煙雨莽蒼蒼，
yān yǔ mǎng cāng cāng

龜蛇鎖大江。
guī shé suǒ dà jiāng

黄鶴知何去？
huáng hè zhī hé qù

剩有遊人處。
shèng yǒu yóu rén chù

把酒酹滔滔，
bǎ jiǔ lèi tāo tāo

心潮逐浪高！
xīn cháo zhú làng gāo

（一九二七年春）

YELLOW CRANE TOWER[1]
to the tune of Buddhist Dancers

Nine streams,[2] mighty and misty, each
    ploughs the land[3] in its course,
One railroad line so endless and dark
    threads from south to north. [4]
Far and wide the smoky rain veils the scene
    and the town,
The Mountain Tortoise[5] and the Mountain
    Snake[6] lock the River Long. [7]

Gone is the crane so yellow and nobody
    knows where,
Now only the tower remains here for visi-
    tors to stare. [8]
I hold up wine to the waves before my
    eyes,
The tides of my heart, too, rise![9]

(Spring 1927)[10]

17

TRANSLATOR'S NOTES

1. Yellow Crane Tower: a very famous tower situated in Wuchang County, Hubei Province. It was first built in the period of the Three Kingdoms (220—280). The present name is said to have come from a tale that a certain immortal once passed by the tower, riding a yellow crane. This poem was first published in *Poetry* (January, 1957).

2. Nine Streams: The Yangzi River branches into many smaller rivers in Hubei and Jiangxi. Here the figure "nine" is only rhetorically used to mean "many". In a letter dated December 29, 1959, to Zhong Xuekun, Mao Zedong says, "Nine streams mean nine rivers in the three provinces of Hunan, Hubei and Jiangxi. However, it is unnecessary to specify each of them; there have been different opinions of the question."

3. the land: the mainland of China.

4. One railroad line: the line from Beijing to Guangzhou.

5. The Mountain Tortoise: the name in the original pronounced as Guishan, located in the city of Hanyang. The mountain looking like a tortoise was believed to be the fossil of an ancient tortoise that once helped the Great King of Yu to regulate rivers and watercourses several thousand years ago.

6. the Mountain Snake: the name in the original pronounced as Sheshan, situated in the city of Wuchang, zigzaging like a snake.

7. the River Long: the Yangzi River, the longest river in China.

8. Gone is the Crane ... for visitors to stare: These two lines al-

18

lude to a poem under the same title "Yellow Crane Tower" by
a Tang poet Cui Hao(? — 755):

The ancient immortal riding the yellow crane goes away,
Here only the Yellow Crane Tower remains today;
The yellow crane is gone and comes back no more,
Only white clouds drift for a thousand years as before.

9. I hold up wine ... my heart, too, rise: On these lines, Mao Zedong offered a comment on December 21, 1958: "It is set in the
eve of the failure of the Great Revolution in 1927; I was very
sad and distracted, quite at a loss what to do. It was in the
spring of the year. Then on August 7 (in the summer of the
year), an urgent meeting was held by the Party, at which, a decision on armed uprising was made, thenceforth, we have had a
way out. "

10. Spring 1927: On April 12, Chiang Kai-shek launched a devas-
tating attack upon the Chinese communists in Shanghai, but
Chen Duxiu, Secretary General of the Central Committee of
the Communist Party of China, instead of staging a counter-
attack against Chiang, insisted on making concession to
Kuomintang and giving up the Party's leadership over the
revolution. Mao Zedong strongly appealed to the Party for an
immediate act to frustrate Chiang's massacre of communists,
but his proposals were ignored and he himself was actually
excluded outside the Party leadership at the Fifth National
Congress of the Communist Party of China held in Wuhan
from April 27 to May 9, 1927.

西 江 月
xī jiāng yuè

井 冈 山
jǐng gāng shān

山下旌旗在望，
shān xià jīng qí zài wàng

山頭鼓角相聞。
shān tóu gǔ jiǎo xiāng wén

敵軍圍困萬千重，
dí jūn wéi kùn wàn qiān chóng

我自巋然不動。
wǒ zì kuī rán bú dòng

早已森嚴壁壘，
zǎo yǐ sēn yán bì lěi

更加衆志成城。
gèng jiā zhòng zhì chéng chéng

黄洋界上炮聲隆，
huáng yáng jiè shàng pào shēng lóng

報道敵軍宵遁。
bào dào dí jūn xiāo dùn

(一九二八年秋)

20

JINGGANG MOUNTAIN[1]

to the tune of Moon
over West River

At the foot of the mountain our banners are
    seen,
On the top our bugles are heard.
Though enemies encircle us in a ring after
    ring,
Nothing can leave us stirred.

Fortified strongly has been our defence,
Our wills united into a wall.
At Huangyangjie[2] the peal of the gun
    comes suddenly thence,
The foe reportedly flees by the dark
    night-pall. [3]

(Autumn 1928)

TRANSLATOR'S NOTES

1. Jinggang Mountain: a tremendous and craggily precipitous mountain, situated at the border of Jiangxi and Hunan Provinces. In October, 1927, the Autumn Harvest Uprising Army led by Mao Zedong drove into the area and set up the first rural revolutionary base. In this area, Mao Zedong mobilized masses to carry on a guerrilla warfare, initiated an agrarian revolution, and established local armed forces, Party organizations, and a workers' and peasants' regime. In April 1928, an army contingent that had participated in the Nanchang Uprising and the contingent of armed peasants that had taken part in the uprisings in Hunan, led by Zhu De and Chen Yi, arrived at the Jinggang Mountains and joined forces with the revolutionary army led by Mao Zedong. After their meeting, these forces were reorganized into the Fourth Army of the Chinese Workers' and Peasants' Red Army, numbering more than 10,000 men. Zhu De served as its commander, Mao Zedong as the Party representative, and Chen Yi as the director of its political department. It was during the period of struggle in the Jinggang Mountains that the principle of the Party's absolute leadership over the army was established. Many fierce battles were fought here; the one referred to in the poem took place in September, 1928.

    This poem was first published in *Poetry* (January 1957).

2. Huangyangjie: the steepest pass of the Jinggang Mountains leading to the Ninggang County of Jiangxi Province, and to the

Ling County of Hunan Province; located in the northwest of the Jinggang Mountains; 1342 feet above the sea level, with deep valleys and gorges; 17 kilometres away from the pass stationed the headquarters of the Red Army.

3. the peal of the gun ... by the dark night-pall: On August 30, 1928, the Red Army repulsed frequent charges on the part of the Kuomintang troops. In the afternoon, some Red Army soldiers found a mortar left behind by the main force of the Red Army and launched a surprising attack upon the Kuomintang troops. Possibly interpreting the peal of the mortar as the token of the return of the main force of the Red Army, the Kuomintang troops quickly withdrew by night.

清 平 樂

qīng píng yuè

蔣桂戰爭

jiǎng guì zhàn zhēng

風雲突變，

fēng yún tū biàn

軍閥重開戰。

jūn fá chóng kāi zhàn

灑向人間都是怨，

sǎ xiàng rén jiān dōu shì yuàn

一枕黃粱再現。

yī zhěn huáng liáng zài xiàn

紅旗躍過汀江，

hóng qí yuè guò tīng jiāng

直下龍岩上杭。

zhí xià lóng yán shàng háng

收拾金甌一片

shōu shí jīn ōu yī piàn

分田分地真忙。

fēn tián fēn dì zhēn máng

（一九二九年秋）

24

THE CLASH BETWEEN CHIANG KAI-SHEK AND WARLORDS IN GUANGXI PROVINCE[1]

to the tune of Music of Peace

The sudden change of wind and rain
Comes when warlords clash again.
Miseries and grievances are heard every-
  where,
For some[2] a Millet Dream[3], for others a
  nightmare.

Red flags[4] leap over the River Tingjiang[5],
Pressing on to Longyan and Shanghang[6].
Part of the Golden Bowl[7] now regained in
  our hand,
The freed men are busy dividing the land[8].

(Autumn 1929)

25

TRANSLATOR'S NOTES

1. The Clash Between Chiang Kai-shek and Warlords in Guangxi Province: At the end of 1928, the Kuomintang Nanking Government proclaimed itself the only legal government of China, thus the contradictions between the warlords under the control of Kuomintang were brought forth to open strife and veiled struggle against each other. On February 21, 1929, Li Zongren and Bai Chongxi, the warlords of Guangxi Province staged a coup d'état in Changsha, driving away Lu Diping, the Pro-Chiang chairman of Hunan Province. On March 26, the Nanking Government issued an order to relieve Li and Bai of their posts. The next day, Chiang Kai-shek sent three armies to assault Wuhan occupied by Guangxi troops. Due to the betrayal on the part of Yang Tenghui, a general under the Guangxi warlords, who was costly bribed by Chiang, the Guangxi warlords army had to withdraw, fleeing southward to Guangxi Province on April 4. Thus ended the clash between Chiang Kai-shek and the warlords of Guangxi Province.

2. some: some warlords.

3. Millet Dream: pipe dream; wishes that cannot be realized. The allusion stems from a story by Shen Jiji, a story-teller in the Tang Dynasty, that a poor scholar named Lu Sheng dreamt that he had become a high official but awoke to find only the pot of millet still cooking on the fire.

4. Red flags: the Red Army.

5. the River Tingjiang: a river originating in Fujian Province and threading through Guangdong Province and flowing southward into the Southern Sea.

6. Longyan and Shanghang: the names of the two counties in the southwest of Fujian Province. On May 19, 1929, the Red Army's Fourth Army started from Ruijin, Jiangxi Province, and came across Tingjiang on May 20. On May 23, June 3 and 19, the Red Army occupied Longyan three times, and on September 21, it occupied Shanghang.

7. the Golden Bowl: the whole land of the country.

8. The freed men are busy dividing the land: From 1929 to 1930, along with the expansion of the rural revolutionary bases, just within the area of 300 li in length and breadth in the west of Fujian Province, the farm lands were distributed to about 800, 000 peasants. The success of the agrarian revolution in the above area is explaind by the fact that frequent clashes between the warlords surely opened up many good chances for the Chinese Communist Party to win the heartfelt support from the peasants by satisfying their needs for cultivated land.

採 桑 子

cǎi sāng zǐ

重 陽

chóng yáng

人生易老天難老,

rén shēng yì lǎo tiān nán lǎo

歲歲重陽。

suì suì chóng yáng

今又重陽,

jīn yòu chóng yáng

戰地黃花分外香。

zhàn dì huáng huā fèn wài xiāng

一年一度秋風勁,

yī nián yī dù qiū fēng jìn

不似春光。

bú sì chūn guāng

勝似春光,

shèng sì chūn guāng

廖廓江天萬里霜。

liáo kuò jiāng tiān wàn lǐ shuāng

(一九二九年十月)

28

THE DOUBLE NINTH[1]
to the tune of Mulberry-
Picking Song

Man ages too easily but heaven never gets
 old,[2]
Double Ninth comes yearly in the same
 mould.
This year's Double Ninth would tell
The yellow flowers[3] on the battlefield[4]
 sweeter smell.[5]

Every year in autumn the wind blows
 with might,
How different from the spring sight!
Yet in splendour the autumn could the
 spring defy
With its frosty and boundless water and
 sky.[6]

(October 1929)

TRANSLATOR'S NOTES

1. The Double Ninth:September 9 in the Chinese lunar calendar. The numeral 9 was worshiped by the Chinese ancients as a Yang figure,i. e. a masculine or positive figure. "September"is the ninth month of the year, thus "September 9" embraces double 9's ——the ninth month and the ninth date. The Double Ninth is a traditional festival day on which people usually ascend a height to enjoy the sight of chrysanthemum. The Double Ninth in 1929 was October 11 in the Gregorian calendar; up to that day, the Red Army led by Mao Zedong had wiped out the local warlords of Tingjiang in the south of Fujian Province and occupied Shanghang. Meanwhile,in the rural revolutionary bases, the agrarian revolution was carried out with great enthusiasm; this meant the overthrow of the landlords and the distribution of land among the peasants.

2. Man ages too easily but heaven never gets old:1)Man's age is shown by his physiological change yet heaven's age bears no discenible traces because its change occurs very slowly;2)That man must get old is a natural law;man dies but the universe exists for ever;3)a possible allusion to a line of the poem"Ode to the Golden Bronze Immortal Who Takes Leave of the Palaces of the Han Dynasty" by Li He(790—816),a Tang poet:"Should heaven be sentimental,old would it be. " The story is told in *Stories of the Three Kingdoms*(Chapter 105) by Luo Guanzhong (?1330—?1400). The allusion is also inserted in Mao Zedong's another poem "The People's Liberation Army

Captures Nanking"(lines 7-8).

3. The yellow flowers:the chrysanthemum flowers. See Note1.

4. the battlefield:the city of Shanghang was just occupied by the Red Army in September of the year.

5. sweeter smell:smell sweeter than usual;believed to suggest a touch of revolutionary optimism.

6. Mao's preference of autumn to spring is often explained by many scholars as 1) autumn is a harvest season;2)autumn is a time when transient things must be killed;3)autumn is a symbol of revolution.

如　夢　令

rú mèng lìng

元　旦

yuán dàn

寧化、清流、歸化，

níng huà qīng liú guī huà

路隘林深苔滑。

lù ài lín shēn tāi huá

今日向何方，

jīn rì xiàng hé fāng

直指武夷山下。

zhí zhǐ wǔ yí shān xià

山下山下，

shān xià shān xià

風展紅旗如畫。

fēng zhǎn hóng qí rú huà

（一九三〇年一月）

NEW YEAR'S DAY[1]

to the tune of
Dream-like Lyric

How hard we passed Ninghua's, Qingliu's,
    Guihua's[2]
Deep woods, slippery moss and a long,
    narrow path![3]
Today whence are we bound?[4]
Straight to the foot of Wuyi,[5] the mount.
The foot, the mount,
The wind unfurls the flags like pictures
    beyond count.

(January 1930)

TRANSLATOR'S NOTES

1. New Year's Day:At the end of 1929,the Kuomintang troops stationed in Jiangxi,Fujian and Guangdong Provinces closed in on the area occupied by the Fourth Army of the Red Army. To preserve its effective strength,the Red Army decided to transfer to the rear area under the Kuomintang rule. A few days later right after the New Year's Day,i. e. January 7,1930,the main force of the Red Army led by Zhu De set out from Gutian,advancing to Jiangxi Province;while Mao Zedong led part of the Red Army covering the evacuation of the main force,going over Wuyi Mountain to Jiangxi via counties like Liancheng,Qingliu,Guihua,and Ninghua.

   This poem was first published in *Poetry*(January,1957).

2. Ninghua,Qingliu,Guihua:three counties in the south of Fujian Province. The order of the three counties is not necessary the actual order in which Mao's troops went through those counties but chiefly out of consideration of certain phonetic requirements on the part of the poet.

3. Deep woods,slippery moss,and a long,narrow path:1)remember it was a rapid and concealed march to shake off the enemy's hot pursuit,thus the Red Army had to choose a narrow path in the remote mountainous district where woods were naturally deep and moss slippery;2)six pauses in the first two lines adroitly employed by the poet to give a sense of sprightly rhythm and forcefulness suggesting the soldiers' vigorous and

brisk strides on the ragged mountain path.

4. Today whence are we bound：Notice the relaxed tone and mood，for the aim of the strategic transfer was finally reached；the enemy by now had been shaken off，so the troops could go straight to the foot of Wuyi Mountain without concealing its movement.

5. Wuyi：a mountain situated in Fujian Province.

减字木兰花
jiǎn zì mù lán huā

廣昌路上
guǎng chāng lù shàng

漫天皆白，
màn tiān jiē bái

雪裏行軍情更迫。
xuě lǐ xíng jūn qíng gèng pò

頭上高山，
tóu shàng gāo shān

風捲紅旗過大關。
fēng juǎn hóng qí guò dà guān

此行何去？
cǐ xíng hé qù

贛江風雪迷漫處。
gàn jiāng fēng xuě mí màn chù

命令昨頒，
mìng lìng zuó bān

十萬工農下吉安。
shí wàn gōng nóng xià jí ān

（一九三〇年二月）

ON THE WAY TO GUANGCHANG COUNTY[1]

to the tune of Lily Magnolia Flowers, Character-Reduced

The whole world is immaculately white,
We march in snow,[2] with hearts and lips
tight. [3]
Above our heads the peaks tower on
high,[4]
Red flags unfurled, the great passes[5] we
pass by!

Now where are we bound?
To the snow-shrouded River Gan. [6]
Yesterday there issued the command:
One hundred thousand armed men[7] should
press on Ji An.

(February 1930)

TRANSLATOR'S NOTES

1. Guangchang County: a county in the southeast of Jiangxi Province, east of Ninghua and Jianning Counties of Fujian Province. From February 2 to 9, 1930, Mao Zedong presided over a military meeting in Potou near Ji An, at which a decision was made to seize the whole area of Jiangxi Province and the first target of attack was Ji An. After the meeting, the Red Army troops pressed forward in several directions to Ji An. The military action, however, was soon rescinded, because the Kuomintang government mustered emergency reinforcements from Hunan, Hubei and Jiangxi Provinces, tending to rescue Ji An from the siege.

   This poem was first published in *People's Literature* (No. 5, 1962).

2. We march in snow: Historical records prove that rare snow-storms happened in Jiangxi in January, 1930, when the Red Army got over the pass at Wuyi Mountain where the local people helped the Red Army soldiers clean up snow and pave the way with chaff.

3. with hearts and lips tight: The earlier text read "with no green cypresses around". Later on, Mao made some correction of the phrase. The present version was rendered according to the author's corrected text in the 1963 edition of *Poems of Chairman Mao* (People's Literature Press, Beijing, 1963).

4. the peaks tower on high: possibly referring to Yunshan Moun-

38

tains abutting on Ningdu County.

5. the great passes: Many passes are seen on the way to Guangchang County: in Yudu County, there are Pingtian Pass, Zuokeng Pass, Niuling Pass; in Ningdu County, there are Donglong Pass, Tianbu Pass, Bailu Pass, Changsheng Pass, Paiyun Pass, Xiuling Pass, and Shituling Pass.

6. River Gan: the biggest river in Jiangxi, branching into two smaller rivers at Ganzhou, hence the name; here vaguely hinting at the area through which the river goes.

7. armed men: The original is "workers and peasants"; the adaptation is made to render a more understandable version from the context to the English-speaking people.

蝶　戀　花

dié liàn huā

從汀州向長沙

cóng tīng zhōu xiàng cháng shā

六月天兵征腐惡，

liù yuè tiān bīng zhēng fǔ è

萬丈長纓要把鯤鵬縛。

wàn zhàng cháng yīng yào bǎ kūn péng fù

贛水那邊紅一角，

gàn shuǐ nà biān hóng yī jiǎo

偏師借重黃公略。

piān shī jiè zhòng huáng gōng lüè

百萬工農齊踴躍，

bǎi wàn gōng nóng qí yǒng yuè

席捲江西直搗湘和鄂。

xí juǎn jiāng xī zhí dǎo xiāng hé è

國際悲歌歌一曲，

guó jì bēi gē gē yī qǔ

狂飆為我從天落。

kuáng biāo wèi wǒ cóng tiān luò

（一九三〇年七月）

MARCH FROM TINGZHOU
TO CHANGSHA[1]

to the tune of Butterflies
Love Flowers

To uproot the corrupt and evil in June God
    sends armies strong[2]
To bind roc and whale[3] with a cord of ten thou-
    sand feet long. [4]
Fiery is the far side of River Gan,[5]
Huang,[6] commander of the wing there, is a tal-
    ented man.

Slaves uprise a million strong, hand in hand,
Sweeping Jiangxi and pressing on Hubei
    and Hunan.
Let's sing the Internationale solemnly in a
    pitch high,
And hail the storm that falls from the sky. [7]

(July 1930)

41

TRANSLATOR'S NOTES

1. March from Tingzhou to Changsha: On June 22, 1930, the First
   Red Army Group stationed in Tingzhou ordered the troops in
   the west of Jiangxi to advance in the direction of Huichang. On
   July 11, another order was issued from the headquarters that
   an attack be staged upon Zhangshu from Xingguo. At 7:30 on
   the afternoon of July 20, the headquarters in Yongfeng gave
   another command that the main force of the Red Army press
   on and gather at Maixie. The poem was chanted during the
   Red Army's march from Tingzhou to Changsha.

   This poem was first published in *People's Literature*
   (May, 1962).

2. God sends armies strong: a metaphor implying armies dedicat-
   ed to a just cause; traditionally emperors and kings in Chinese
   history called their armies "God-sent armies". Here Mao Zedong uses the metaphor to mean the Red Army.

3. roc and whale: an allusion from *Zhuang Zi*: "There is fish
   called Kun in the Northern Sea; it is as long as stretching several thousand li. When the roc changes into the bird called
   Peng, it has a back as wide as stretching several thousand li;
   when it is flying, its wings are like longtrailed, sky-covering
   clouds. " Roc and whale refer to Peng and Kun respectively;
   the version is understood here as a compromise of the original, symbolizing Kuomintang chiefs, headed by Chiang Kai-
   shek.

4. a cord of ten thousand feet long: According to *History of Han Dynasty*, LXIV, a young man called Zhong Jun recommended himself to go and persuade the king of Yue in the south to subject to the Han Dynasty. He said, if he were given a long cord, he could bind the king of Yue in the south with it and take the king right to the palaces of Han. Here in the poem, Mao uses the cord to indicate the military strength of the Red Army.

5. Fiery is the far side of River Gan: "Fiery" implies the influence of the Red Army. "River Gan" here means the district around the city of Nanchang down the River Gan where the battle was fought by the Sixth Army of the Red Army to capture the city.

6. Huang: Huang Gonglüe (1898—1931), a native of the Xiangxiang County, Hunan Province; commander of the Sixth Army of the Red Army. In June, 1930, the Sixth Army was in the southwest of Jiangxi while the main force of the Red Army, i. e. the Fourth and Twelfth Armies, were moving from Fujian to Jiangxi, thus the Sixth Army functioned as the wing of the main force.

7. the storm that falls from the sky: See Du Fu "Seven Poems Written in the Year of Qianyuan when I Lived in the Tonggu County": "The sad wind falls for me from the sky." In Mao's poem, "storm" symbolizes the rebellion led by the Communist Party that took place in Jiangxi and Hunan at that time.

漁 家 傲

yú jiā ào

反第一次大"圍剿"

fǎn dì yī cì dà wéi jiǎo

萬木霜天紅爛漫，

wàn mù shuāng tiān hóng làn màn

天兵怒氣冲霄漢。

tiān bīng nù qì chōng xiāo hàn

霧滿龍岡千嶂暗，

wù mǎn lóng gāng qiān zhàng àn

齊聲喚，

qí shēng huàn

前頭捉了張輝瓚。

qián tóu zhuō le zhāng huī zàn

二十萬軍重入贛，

èr shí wàn jūn chóng rù gàn

風煙滾滾來天半。

fēng yān gǔn gǔn lái tiān bàn

喚起工農千百萬，

huàn qǐ gōng nóng qiān bǎi wàn

AGAINST THE FIRST "ENCIRCLEMENT" CAMPAIGN[1]
to the tune of Fishermen's Pride

Maple trees are burning red[2] under the
    frosty sky,[3]
The heaven army's wrath[4] now soars to the
    clouds on high.
Mist envelops Longgang[5] and thousand
    peaks blurred,
Cries in one voice are suddenly heard:
At the front Zhang Huizan falls a jail bird.

Two hundred thousand strong invade
    Jiangxi once more,[6]
The billowing dust and the wicked wind
    from the mid-sky pour.
Ah, workers and peasants, rise in millions
    with your head high!
Fight as we do now,

同心幹，

tóng xīn gàn

不周山下紅旗亂。〔原注〕

bù zhōu shān xià hóng qí luàn

（一九三一年春）

〔原注〕關於共工頭觸不周山的故事：

《淮南子·天文訓》："昔者共工與顓頊争為帝，怒而觸不周之山，天柱折，地維絶。天傾西北，故日月星辰移焉；地不滿東南，故水潦塵埃歸焉。"

《國語·周語》："昔共工棄此道也，虞于湛樂，淫失其身，欲壅防百川，墮高堙庳，以害天下。皇天弗福，庶民弗助，禍亂並興，共工用滅。"（韋昭注："賈侍中〔按指後漢賈逵〕云："共工，諸侯，炎帝之後，姜姓也。顓頊氏衰，共工氏侵陵諸侯，與高辛氏争而王也。"）

《史記》司馬貞補《三皇本紀》："當其（按指女媧）末年也，諸侯有共工氏，任智刑以强，霸而不王，以水乘木，乃與祝融戰，不勝而怒，乃頭觸不周山崩，天柱折，地維缺。"

毛按：諸説不同。我取《淮南子·天文訓》，共工是勝利的英雄。你看，"怒而觸不周之山，天柱折，地維絶。天傾西北，故日月星辰移焉；地不滿東南，故水潦塵埃歸焉。"他死了没有呢？没有説。看來是没有死，共工是確實勝利了。

Lo ! At the foot of Mount Buzhou, red flags flutter and fly. *

(Spring 1931)

* AUTHOR'S NOTE:

The story about Gonggong[7] butting against Mount Buzhou:
"On Astronomy" in *Huai Nan Zi* says:"In ancient times Gonggong and Zhuanxu fought each other for the throne. In a fit of
rage Gonggong butted against Mount Buzhou, breaking the pillars of heaven and snapping the ties of the earth. Then the sky
shifted towards the northwest, tilting the sun, moon and stars;
the earth sank in the southeast so that dust and water gathered
there. "

"The Chronicle of Zhou"in *Guoyu* says:"In ancient times
Gonggong, departing from the right way, gave himself up to pleasure and unbridled licence. He tried to stem the hundred streams,
destroy hills and silt up low places, and thus brought disasters to
the earth. Heaven did not give its blessing, nor the people their
help. Calamities and troubles broke out and Gonggong perished. "
The ancient commentator Wei Zhao quotes from the Palace Officer Jia, i. e. , Jia Kui of the Later Han Dynasty:"Gonggong was
the lord of Jiang clan, a descendant of the Fiery Emperor. When
Emperor Zhuanxu's power was on the decline, Gonggong attacked other vassal lords and fought Gaoxin for the throne. "

In "The Annals of the Three Emperors", Sima Zhen's addenda to Sima Qian's *The Recordings of History*, it is said: "Towards the end of her (Nü Wa's) reign, a lord named Gonggong became powerful through his resourcefulness and the severe discipline he enforced. He did not rule like a king but like an autocrat. Representing the element of water, he wanted to succeed Nü Wa who represented the element of wood. He fought Zhu Rong and was defeated. In a fit of rage he knocked his head against Mount Buzhou, so that the pillars of heaven were broken and the ties of the earth torn. "

These are the different versions of the legend. I prefer the version in *Huai Nan Zi*, which presents Gonggong as a victorious hero. Please notice this: "In a fit of rage Gonggong butted against Mount Buzhou, breaking the pillars of heaven and snapping the ties of the earth. Then the sky shifted towards the northwest, tilting the sun, moon and stars; the earth sank in the southeast so that dust and water gathered there. " Did Gonggong perish in the attempt? *Huai Nan Zi* is silent on this question. We may take that he did not, but came out victorious. (The English version of this note is taken, with slight changes, from the 1976 edition of *Mao Tsetung Poems*, Peking: Foreign Languages Press, p. 23.)

48

TRANSLATOR'S NOTES

1. Against the First "Encirclement"Campaign: In October,1930, Chiang Kai-shek ended the wars against Feng Yuxiang and Yan Xishan,two warlords,and then in December,Chiang flew to Nanchang to deploy his first encirclement campaign against the Red Army, appointing Lu Diping, Chairman of Jiangxi Province, as the Commander-in-Chief, and Zhang Huizan, the commander of the eighteenth division,as the field commander. Chiang employed about 100, 000 men, divided into eight columns, to advance southward from Ji'an-Jianning line against the Red Army's base area. The Red Army had about 40,000 men and was concentrated in the area of Huangpi and Xiaobu in Ningdu County,Jiangxi Province. The situation was as follows. The encirclement forces did not exceed 100, 000 men,none of whom were Chiang Kai-shek's own troops,and the general situation was not very grave. The enemy division under Luo Lin,defending Ji'an,was located across the Gan River to the west. The three enemy divisions under Gong Bing-fan,Zhang Huizan and Tan Daoyuan had advanced and occupied Futian-Donggu-Longgang-Yuantou sector southeast of Ji' an and northwest of Ningdu. The main body of Zhang Huizan's division was at Longgang and that of Tan Daoyuan's division at Yuantou. The two divisions under Zhang Huizan and Tan Daoyuan made up the enemy's main force,thus,if the Red Army attacked one division at a time it would enjoy absolute superiority. For these reasons and others,Mao Zedong de-

49

cided that the first battle should be against Zhang Huizan's main force. The Red Army successfully hit two of his brigades and his divisional headquarters, capturing the entire force of nine thousand men and the divisional commander himself, without letting a single man escape. This victory scared Tan's division into fleeing towards Dongshao and Xu's division into fleeing towards Toupi. The Red Army then pursued Tan's division and wiped out half of it. Two battles were fought in five days, and, fearing to be defeated, Chiang's forces in Futian, Donggu and Toupi retreated in disorder. So ended the first campaign of "encirclement and suppression" against the Red Army. (See *Selected Works of Mao Tse-tung*, Vol. 1, Peking: Foreign Languages Press, 1977, pp. 226-227.)

2. burning red: a pun, implying the red leaves of the maple trees and the Red Army soldiers who usually wore red stars on their caps, red collar insignias and red armbands, identical with the red flags of the Army.

3. the frosty sky: usually referring to autumn as in Mao's another poem "Changsha ——to the tune of Spring Beaming in Garden"(For freedom all creatures with each other vie, /Under the frosty and vaulted sky), but here it indicates the winter. In China, both in winter and autumn, frost can be seen.

4. The heaven army's wrath: the morale of the Red Army men.

5. Longgang: a small town in Yongfeng County, Jiangxi Province.

6. Two hundred thousand strong invade Jiangxi once more: No-

tice the second stanza of the poem is about the second encirclement and suppression campaign against the Red Army. On April 1, 1931, Chiang Kai-shek mustered the suppression forces numbering 200,000 under the command of He Yingqin to prey on the Red Army occupied area. For details, see note to "Against the Second 'Encirclement' Campaign —— to the tune of Fishermen's Pride".

7. Gonggong: a tribe chief in Chinese ancient tales. Since Mao Zedong regards Gonggong as a hero, it is only too natural for him to use the name Gonggong to allude to the Chinese Communist Party and the Red Army, because the Chinese character "Gong" (meaning "common", "together", "all", etc.) in "Gonggong" and that in "Gongchandang" (the Communist Party) are the same both in spelling and pronunciation. Mao obviously takes great pains to effect a pun by employing this historical story.

漁 家 傲
yú jiā ào

反第二次大"圍剿"
fǎn dì èr cì dà wéi jiǎo

白雲山頭雲欲立，
bái yún shān tóu yún yù lì

白雲山下呼聲急，
bái yún shān xià hū shēng jí

枯木朽株齊努力。
kū mù xiǔ zhū qí nǔ lì

槍林逼，
qiāng lín bī

飛將軍自重霄入。
fēi jiāng jūn zì chóng xiāo rù

七百里驅十五日，
qī bǎi lǐ qū shí wǔ rì

贛水蒼茫閩山碧，
gàn shuǐ cāng máng mǐn shān bì

橫掃千軍如捲蓆。
héng sǎo qiān jūn rú juǎn xí

52

AGAINST THE SECOND "ENCIRCLEMENT" CAMPAIGN[1]

to the tune of Fishermen's Pride

On top of White Cloud Mountain[2], clouds
    mount a thunderhead[3],
At its foot rallying cries[4] burst forth from
    the battle red. [5]
Withered trees and rotten stumps[6] all fight,
    in spirits high.
Suddenly a forest of rifles presses nearby,
While the flying general[7] swoops down
    from the sky.

Fifteen days see a rapid march of seven
    hundred li,[8]
Vast are waters in Gan[9], and green are
    mountains in Min,[10]
Like rolling back a mat we sweep off the
    armies we see.

有人泣，
yǒu rén qì

為營步步嗟何及！
wéi yíng bù bù jiē hé jí

（一九三一年夏）

Someone[11] is heard to wail ——

His strategy "Entrench at every step" is
bitterly fated to fail.

(Summer 1931)

TRANSLATOR'S NOTES

1. Against the Second "Encirclement" Campaign: In February,
   1931, Chiang Kai-shek appointed He Yingqin as the commander of a large army numbering 200,000 men to launch an all-
   out offensive against the Red-Army-occupied area. As in the
   first encirclement campaign, none of the forces were Chiang
   Kai-shek's own troops. Among them the 19th Route Army
   under Cai Tingkai, the 26th under Sun Lianzhong and the 8th
   under Zhu Shaoliang were strong, while all the rest were
   rather weak. The Red Army (numbering over 30,000 men)
   was somewhat smaller than in the first campaign, but it had
   had four months in which to recuperate and build up energy.
   The Red Army thus attacked the Futian sector first, defeating
   the forces of Wang Jinyu, and of Gong Bingfan (totalling 11
   regiments). Then the Red Army swept across to the east, at-
   tacking the forces of Guo Huazong, Sun Lianzhong, Zhu Shaoliang and Liu Heding in succession. "In fifteen days (from May
   16 to May 30, 1931) we marched seven hundred li, fought five
   battles, captured more than twenty thousand rifles and roundly smashed the enemy's 'encirclement and suppression' campaign" (Mao Zedong, *Selected Works of Mao Tse-tung*, vol. 1,

Peking:Foreign Languages Press,1977,pp. 227-228.)

2. White Cloud Mountain:a mountain located in the southeast of Ji'an County,Jiangxi Province. White clouds are said to have been always veiling the mountain,hence the name.

3. Clouds mount a thunderhead:a metaphor implying both the angry clouds and the angry Red Army men share a bitter hatred of the enemy.

4. rallying cries:shouts of the enemy.

5. the battle red:the red-hot battle.

6. withered trees and rotten stumps:Explanations of the phrase are too many to numerate;here are some of them:1)all the masses, workers and peasants, are mobilized into fighting (*People's Daily*,May 12,1962);2)the fleeing enemy's suspision of danger in all things;even the withered trees and rotten stumps seem to be armed soldiers(Ibid);3)an allusion to Sima Xiangru's "Remonstration with Hunting": "All the withered trees and rotten stumps become evils. "Thus the phrase refers to the enemy(*People's Daily*,June 8,1962);4)an allusion to Zou Yang's "Self-Vindication in Prison to His Majesty,the King of Liangxiao": "If praised beforehand,even the withered trees and rotten stumps can perform meritorious deeds and find favour with his Majesty. "

7. the flying general:a very brave and skillful general named Li Guang in the Han Dynasty. See Sima Qian's *The Recordings of History*: "When Huns heard that Li Guang and his troops stationed at Youbeiping,they called him 'The Flying General' of

56

the Han Dynasty, avoiding any confrontation with him for a few years, being afraid to intrude on Youbeiping."The phrase here is used to stand for the Red Army soldiers.

8. See Note 1 above.

9. Gan: the short form for Jiangxi Province.

10. Min: the short form for Fujian Province. This line drops a hint that battles took place in this district.

11. Someone: Chiang Kai-shek.

菩薩蠻
pú sà mán

大 柏 地
dà bǎi dì

赤橙黄緑青藍紫，
chì chéng huáng lǜ qīng lán zǐ

誰持彩練當空舞？
shuí chí cǎi liàn dāng kōng wǔ

雨後復斜陽，
yǔ hòu fù xié yáng

關山陣陣蒼。
guān shān zhèn zhèn cāng

當年鏖戰急，
dāng nián áo zhàn jí

彈洞前村壁。
dàn dòng qián cūn bì

裝點此關山，
zhuāng diǎn cǐ guān shān

今朝更好看。
jīn zhāo gèng hǎo kàn

（一九三三年夏）

58

DABODI[1]
to the tune of Buddhist Dancers

Violet, blue, orange, yellow, indigo, red and
  green——[2]
Who dances with the colour ribbon[3] in the
  sky serene?
Newly over is the rain, there appears the
  sun setting again,
Now greener are the passes[4] and hills in a
  view so plain.

Years ago a battle was fought here tooth
  and nail,
The village walls[5] were riddled with bullets
  like a hail.
The past battleground is adorned by the
  scars from war,
Now it looks far more fair than it was before.

(Summer 1933)

TRANSLATOR'S NOTES

1. Dabodi: a place situated sixty li away north of the city of Rui-jin, Jiangxi Province. In early June, 1929, the Kuomintang troops (numbering 30,000 men) stationed in Hunan and Jiangxi were going to launch the third encirclement and suppression campaign against the Red-Army-occupied area in Jinggang Mountains. In order to break through the Kuomintang suppression campaign and to obtain enough supplies and clothing for the winter, the main force (numbering 3600 men) of the Fourth Red Army led by Mao Zedong, Zhu De and Chen Yi, left Jinggang Mountains and advanced in the direction of southern Jiangxi on January 14. Having come under attack from all sides, the Fourth Red Army suffered military reverses in five battles on the way. But on February 10, things offered a favourable turn to the Red Army; on that day, Mao Zedong and his comrades-in-arms deployed an ambush ring at Mazi Col near Dabodi, inflicting heavy losses on the enemy force under the command of Liu Shiyi who was hot on the trail of the Red Army. The battle was so fierce that Chen Yi later on wrote of it as "the most honourable battle ever since the birth of the Red Army."

   In the summer of 1933, Mao Zedong revisited Dabodi; the memory of the battle there inspired him into composing the poem above.

   This poem was first published in *Poetry* (January 1957).

2. Violet, blue, orange, yellow, indigo, red and green: the seven

60

colours of rainbow; notice here the original order of the colour arrangement is red, orange, yellow, green, indigo, blue and violet. The change of the order comes from a need for better rhythm and rhyme in the English version.

3. the colour ribbon: the rainbow.

4. the Passes: referring to Mazi Col and mountain peaks nearby, south of Dabodi. This place was given a new name Guanshan in memory of the battle many years ago(1929).

5. The village walls... a hail: During the Culture Revolution, in the walls of the Dengkeng Village near the battle-ground, bullet heads were found and the village was thus changed its name into the Qian Village; Qian means "advance", "front", etc.

清 平 樂

qīng píng yuè

會 昌

huì chāng

東方欲曉，

dōng fāng yù xiǎo

莫道君行早。

mò dào jūn xíng zǎo

踏遍青山人未老，

tà biàn qīng shān rén wèi lǎo

風景這邊獨好。

fēng jǐng zhè biān dú hǎo

會昌城外高峰，

huì chāng chéng wài gāo fēng

顛連直接東溟。

diān lián zhí jiē dōng míng

戰士指看南粵，

zhàn shì zhǐ kàn nán yuè

更加鬱鬱葱葱。

gèng jiā yù yù cōng cōng

（一九三四年夏）

62

HUICHANG[1]
to the tune of Music of Peace

The day will soon break in the east,
Say not "You are an early bird to start".
Having tranversed all the hills[2] I am not
    old[3] in the least,
Only to find the scenery here plays the
    fairest part.

Rising and falling from outside the city
    walls of Huichang,
To the east seas the mountains ranges run.
Our soldiers point southward to East and
    West Guang[4],
Where the southern hills look doubly ver-
    dant and young.

(Summer 1934)

TRANSLATOR'S NOTES

1. Huichang: a county in the southeast corner of Jiangxi Province.

   In January 1931, Wang Ming (originally known as Chen Shaoyu, 1904-1974) assumed leadership in the Chinese Communist Party at the Fourth Plenary Session of its Sixth Central Committee. Mao Zedong thought that, from that time to 1934, Wang Ming promoted within the Party a "Left" opportunist line characterized by doctrinairism, which did great damage to the revolution; that Wang stubbornly insisted on the seizing of big cities and opposed the strategy of encircling the cities from the countryside and seizing power by armed forces; that Wang and his like wanted the Red Army to occupy the major cities immediately and ordered the staging of strikes and demonstrations by workers and students in the large cities controled by Kuomintang; that, as a result, nearly all the Party organizations in the Kuomintang areas were destroyed; that Wang and his followers adopted a policy of "ruthless struggle" and "merciless blows" towards those comrades who disagreed with him. Mao Zedong himself actually was at one time squeezed out of the leadership position in the Red Army.

   In October 1933, Chiang Kai-shek mobilized one million men to conduct the fifth "encirclement and suppression" campaign against the Central Revolutionary Base and the neighbouring Hunan-Jiangxi and Fujian-Zhejiang-Jiangxi bases. Because of the "Left" opportunists' opposition to what they called "guerrillaism", the flexible tactics of concentrating a superior force, luring the enemy deep into our territory and conducting a mobile warfare were abandoned. As the Red Army was forced to fight pitched battles against a much superior enemy, it found itself in a passive position and , despite one year of struggle, failed to thwart the enemy's "encirclement and suppression" campaign and had to leave the Central Revolutionary Base for a strategic shift. In October 1934, the Red Army's First Front Army (also known as the Central Red Army) of 80,000 men left Changting and Ninghua of Fujian, and Ruijin and Yudu of Jiangxi to begin the Long March.

In the summer of 1934, more than two months before the beginning of the Long March Mao Zedong arrived at Huichang and attended a meeting there. At the daybreak of July 23, Mao and his men ascended the Huichang Mountain (also named Lanshanling) situated northwest of Huichang where Mao wrote the above poem.

On December 21, 1958, Mao Zedong made a note to the poem:"In 1934, the situation was critical, and the Long March was under preparation; I felt rather gloomy then. This piece of 'Music of Peace' along with that piece of 'Buddhist Dancers (Yellow Crane Tower)' was the very revelation of my mood at that time. " (See *Appreciation of Poems by Mao Zedong*, Jiangsu Classical Books Press, 1990, p. 48.)

This poem was first published in *Poetry* (January 1957).

2. Having traversed all green hills: Ever since the 1927 Autumn

Harvest Uprising, Mao Zedong and his men left their traces in many mountains and hills scattered in Hunan, Jiangxi, Fujian and Guangdong Provinces.

3. I am not old: Mao was fourty years old then.

4. East and West Guang: historically referring to Guangdong and Guangxi; here chiefly to Guangdong.

东方欲晓，莫道君行早。踏遍青山人未老，风景这边独好。

会昌城外高峰，颠连直接东溟。战士指看南粤，更加郁郁葱葱。

调寄清平乐

一九三四年夏

十六字令三首

shí liù zì lìng sān shǒu

山，

shān

快馬加鞭未下鞍。

kuài mǎ jiā biān wèi xià ān

驚回首，

jīng huí shǒu

離天三尺三[原注]。

lí tiān sān chǐ sān

其 二

qí   èr

山，

shān

倒海翻江捲巨瀾。

dǎo hǎi fān jiāng juǎn jù lán

奔騰急，

bēn téng jí

萬馬戰猶酣。

wàn mǎ zhàn yóu hān

THREE DITTIES

to the tune of
Sixteen-Character Ditty[1]

1

Oh peak!

Whip and spur, I ride my horse and over
fly,

In surprise turning my head I shriek:

The heaven is only three feet and three
inches high! *[2]

2

Oh peaks!

All bristle like surging waves in a careening
sea beyond,[3]

Like ten thousand steeds[4]

Galloping in fury on the battle-ground.

3

Oh peaks!

其 三

qí sān

山，

shān

刺破青天鍔未殘。

cì pò qīng tiān è wèi cán

天欲墮，

tiān yù duò

賴以拄其間。

lài yǐ zhǔ qí jiān

（一九三四年——一九三五年）

〔原注〕民謠：上有骷髏山，

下有八寶山，

離天三尺三。

人過要低頭，

馬過要下鞍。

Piercing the blue your points sharp remain!
The sky nearly falls with leaks,
And you like pillars it sustain.

(1934-1935)[5]

* AUTHOR'S NOTE

A folk rhyme runs:

Up above is Skull Mountain,
Down below is Eight-treasure Mountain,
The sky is three feet and three inches high,
Lower your head if you on foot go by,
Dismount if you ride a horse on the fly.

71

TRANSLATOR'S NOTES

1. In surprise turning my head I shriek:/The heaven is only three feet and three inches high: 1) The rider, after flying over the mountain top, feels surprised when he notices the distance between the top and the heaven is only three feet and three inches high; 2) the rider goes past the foot of the mountain and exclaimes for the height of the mountain when he turns his head to look at the top.

2. All bristle like surging waves in a careening sea beyond: 1) All the mountains are like surging waves in the sea; 2) the Red Army men are marching and fighting in the wave-like mountains (*Languages Studies*, No. 8, 1957).

3. Like ten thousand steeds/Galloping in fury on the battle-ground: 1) (Mountains are) like racing steeds on the battle-ground; 2) steeds are likened to the Red Army soldiers who are fighting against the enemy heroically (*Languages Teaching*, No. 10, 1958); 3) the galloping steeds are the images of mountains as well as the Red Army men advancing and fighting in the mountains (*Annotations and Notes to Chairman Mao's Poems*, People's Press, 1967, P. 47).

4. Oh Peaks! ... like pillars it sustain: 1) This poem only describes the loftiness and magnificence of the mountains without reference to men, the first two lines depicting the sharpness of the mountains' tops; the last two lines describing the power and grandeur of the mountains; 2) the mountains in

this poem refer to the Chinese Communist Party and the Red Army; 3) the poem describes both the mountains and the revolutionaries. Mao used to saying: Heaven can never fall. Then why does he say in the poem "The sky nearly falls?" It is an irony, meaning even if the sky falls, we can hold it up. (See *Learning Language*, No. 1, March, 1960.)

5. 1934-1935: during the period of the Long March. These three poems, though having a theme and an artistic form in common, were written in different times after the Zunyi Conference. The first was written in December, 1934 when the Red Army marched towards Guizhou. The two mountains, Skull Mountain and Treasure Mountain, mentioned in the author's note, are just situated in the Leishan County, Guizhou Province.

The second poem was possibly written before June, 1935, when the Red Army marched through the border of Yunnan, Guizhou and Sichuan Provinces.

The third poem was written possibly after February and before October, 1935, because it is put between "Loushan Pass" and "Long March" in the editions of *Poems of Chairman Mao* revised by Mao himself (*Tentative Interpretations of Poems of Chairman Mao*, ed. Chinese Department of Fujian Normal University, 1977, pp. 123-124).

憶秦娥
yì qín é

婁山關
lóu shān guān

西風烈，
xī fēng liè

長空雁叫霜晨月。
cháng kōng yàn jiào shuāng chén yuè

霜晨月，
shuāng chén yuè

馬蹄聲碎，喇叭聲咽。
mǎ tí shēng suì lǎ bā shēng yè

雄關漫道真如鐵，
xióng guān màn dào zhēn rú tiě

而今邁步從頭越。
ér jīn mài bù cóng tóu yuè

從頭越，
cóng tóu yuè

蒼山如海，殘陽如血。
cāng shān rú hǎi cán yáng rú xuè

（一九三五年二月）

74

LOUSHAN PASS[1]

to the tune of Recall a Qin Beauty

Strong is the west wind that wails,[2]
Under the frosty morning moon
    a crying wild goose sails.[3]
Under the frosty morning moon
Horses trotting,
Bugles sobbing.[4]

Tell me not the great pass
    is iron wall kissing cloud,
Now we are crossing its summit
    with strides proud.
Crossing its summit,
The setting sun is bloodily red seen,
The vast sea of mountains green.[5]

(February 1935)

TRANSLATOR'S NOTES

1. Loushan Pass: a pass situated north of the Great Loushan
   Mountain near Zunyi, Guizhou Province; it is steep, perilous
   and strategically located, historically a key pass for many military actions. During the Long March, the Red Army twice
   seized the pass respectively in Jan. and Feb. 1935.

2. In October 1934, with the failure of thwarting Chiang Kai-
   shek's fifth "encirclement and suppression" campaign, the Red
   Army withdrew from the Central Revolutionary Base and began the Long March. Breaking through four rings of block-
   ade, the Red Army went through Guangdong, Hunan and
   Guangxi to enter Guizhou. During the Long March, the Red
   Army found itself in danger time and again and it suffered
   heavy casualties until only less than 50 per cent of its men re-
   mained.

   In January 1935, the Party's Central Committee convened
   an enlarged meeting of its Political Bureau in Zunyi, Guizhou
   Province. During the meeting, Wang Ming's military line
   labled as "Left" opportunism was criticised and, instead, Mao
   Zedong's military line was fully established. The leadership
   structure of the Party was reorganized, and Mao Zedong,
   Zhou Enlai, and Wang Jiaxiang were elected as members of
   the leading group in charge of military affairs. The meeting also established Mao Zedong's leading position in the Party.

   After the Zunyi Conference, the Red Army entered
   northwestern Sichuan where it joined forces with the Fourth

Front Army under the command of Zhang Guotao who was later on criticised for his activities of splitting the Red Army; the Army thus continued its northward march. After enduring tremendous hardship and suffering numerous setbacks, the Red Army finally arrived at the base area in northern Shaanxi in October 1935. There it joined forces with the local Red Army troops. The Long March covering 12,500 kilometres is, indeed, unprecedented not only in the military history of China but also in that of the world.

3. Strong is the west wind ... a crying wild goose sails: 1) These two lines describe the scene seen by the Red Army when they pressed forward to Loushan Pass; 2) the description is not about how the Red Army men were marching on to Loushan Pass but about the atmosphere of the battle-ground when the Red Army soldiers were fiercely fighting.

4. Under the frosty morning noon ... Bugles sobbing: 1) These three lines describe the urgency of the task and sternness of the military order; no human voice was heard but wind, horse and bugles; 2) the bugles' sound was lowered (sobbing) in case the enemy should know the whereabouts of the Red Army; 3) "trotting" and "sobbing" are good descriptions of the tragic solemnity of the attack staged by the Red Army cavalry.

5. There are heated disscussions over the time at which Mao wrote the poem and over some other points; the following are listed the essential arguments: 1) In January 1935, the Red Army starting from Zunyi went through Loushan Pass, and

77

on February 25 of the same year, the Red Army returned to Zunyi via Loushan Pass a second time, thus the poem is believed to write about the things which respectively happened in two periods of time. The first stanza is set in the autumn of 1934 when the Red Army began its Long March. The second stanza is set in January, 1935 when the Red Army resumed its Long March after the Zunyi Conference. So what happens in the poem is not on the same day; 2) what is written about in the poem does happen on the same day. The first stanza describes the battle atmosphere, while the second about the heroism of the Red Army men when they have conquered the enemy. True, the Red Army went over Loushan Pass twice, but only the second time Witnessed the fierce battle. To say "the great pass is iron wall" implies at least two things. First, the pass is very precipitous and impregnable; second, the pass must have been firmly entrenched. And, indeed, we know, Loushan Pass then was held fast by the four Kuomintang regiments. Thus the line "The setting sun is bloodily red seen" can be interpretated as a symbol of the bloody fight for the capture of the pass; 3) "the frosty morning" and "the setting sun" clearly indicate what is written in the poem happens on the same day. The belief that "the first stanza is set in the autumn of 1934" is wrong, because it is impossible for Mao Zedong to write about Loushan Pass in the autumn of 1934 when the Red Army did not even reach the pass. Actually, on the morning of January 8, 1935, the Red Army men seized the pass without much fighting, that is to say, the victory was not so bloodily won. What is more important is that

Mao Zedong could not have been in the army there, for, on the afternoon of January 8, 1935, Mao was present, and spoke to the masses, at a "Ten Thousand People Meeting" held in the city of Zunyi; meanwhile, on the same day, Mao Zedong took part in the Zunyi Conference of historic significance, at which Mao was elected Chairman of the Central Committee of the Chinese Communist Party. Mao appeared at two meetings on the single day, he could not have been to Loushan Pass at the same time, therefore the poem is not about the first fight for the capture of the pass. The second fight for the capture of Loushan Pass took place from the evening of February 25 till the daybreak of February 26; Mao was in the army, but he did not go through the pass. It was on February 19 that Mao went over the pass, yet this time, no fighting happened. So it is now clear that the poem "Loushan Pass" was written on February 19, 1935; and what is written is not about the fighting scene supposed to happen at Loushan Pass but about the scene of Loushan Pass Mao saw and felt about on that day.

七　律
qī　　lù

長　征
cháng　　zhēng

紅軍不怕遠征難，
hóng jūn bú pà yuǎn zhēng nán

萬水千山只等閒。
wàn shuǐ qiān shān zhǐ děng xián

五嶺逶迤騰細浪，
wǔ lǐng wēi yí téng xì làng

烏蒙磅礴走泥丸。
wū méng páng bó zǒu ní wán

金沙水拍雲崖暖，
jīn shā shuǐ pāi yún yá nuǎn

大渡橋橫鐵索寒。
dà dù qiáo héng tiě suǒ hán

更喜岷山千里雪，
gèng xǐ mín shān qiān lǐ xuě

三軍過後盡開顏。
sān jūn guò hòu jìn kāi yán

（一九三五年十月）

80

THE LONG MARCH[1]
to the tune of Seven-Character Lü Shi

The red army regards the Long March as
    nothing but a game,
Ten thousand mountains and rivers[2] are
    easy for them to tame.
Like foamy ripples the Five Ridges[3] stretch
    in an unbroken chain;
Like mud balls[4] the majestic Wumeng
    Ranges[5] roll by without reign.

The waves of Golden Sand[6] buffet warm
    the towering cliffs,[7]
The iron-chain bridge spanning the Dadu
    River with cold stiffs. [8]
When crossing the Min Mountains[9] covered
    with boundless snow,
Smiling are the three Armies[10] and all faces
    happily glow.

                      (October 1935)

TRANSLATOR'S NOTES

1. The Long March: See Note 2 to "Loushan Pass".

2. Ten thousand mountains and rivers: countless mountains and rivers; typical of the Chinese rhetorical figure to mean many, manifold and countless.

3. the Five Ridges: the Dayu Ridge, the Qitian Ridge, the Dupang Ridge, the Mengzhu Ridge and the Yuecheng Ridge. These five ridges span the borders of five provinces: Jiangxi, Hunan, Guangdong, Guangxi and Guizhou.

4. like mud balls: 1) Wumeng Ranges looked like mud balls from the view of an observer (Mao) who stood high at the top of a mountain; 2) mud balls are compared to the Red Army men who threaded through the mountains (*Language and Literature*, No. 3, 1959; No. 2, 1960); 3) the Red Army men crossed the great mountains just like crossing small mud balls (*Language and Literature*, No. 4, 1959); 4) mud balls and low hills, to be corroborated by Mao's another poem "Loushan Pass" in which Mao likens mountains to the vast sea (*Language Teaching*, No. 2, 1960); 5) the note 1) ignores the epic atmosphere and hardship embodied in the poem (*Poetry*, No. 2, 1958); 6) the metaphor "mud balls" comes not from *History of the Han Dynasty* by Ban Gu(32-92) but from *The History of the Later Han Dynasty* by Fan Ye(398-445): "Wang Yuan said to Wei Xiao: Please let me use a mud ball to clog up the Hangu Pass for your majesty." The Hangu Pass is a very

perilous place: if one guard is there, ten thousand invaders cannot get over (*Language Teaching*, No. 4, 1959); 7) no matter how majestic the Wumeng Ranges are, they are like mud balls under the feet of the Red Army men; it is mountains that roll by like mud balls under men's feet not that men climb the mud-ball-like mountains.

5. Wumeng Ranges: mountains stretching across Yunnan and Guizhou.

6. Golden Sand: the Golden Sand River, the upper reaches of the Yangzi River, down to Yibin, junction point with the Min River, in Sichuan Province; but here referring to the upper course going through Yunnan Province.

7. buffet warm the towering cliffs: the waves of the Golden Sand River Constantly strike the towering cliffs, giving people a feeling of warmth (*Language Learning*, No. 6, 1957).

8. with cold stiffs: stiffs with cold. When the iron-chain bridge spans the river, the spanning itself gives one a very strong sense of cold and stiffness (*Journal of Shandong University*, No. 3, 1959).

9. Min Mountains: mountains located along the border of Sichuan Province.

10. the three Armies: 1) traditionally meaning the whole army of a country, written as the Three Armies; 2) in the Zhou Dynasty (11. B. C. -3. B. C.), there was a three-army system: A big country owned Three Armies; a small country owned Two Armies or only One Army; 3) the three Armies here

mean a) the Red Army as a whole including the First Red Army, the Second Red Army and the Fourth Red Army; b) the First Red Army in particular yet with reference to the Second and Fourth Red Armies, because when the First Red Army got over the Min Mountains in June 1935, the rest two armies were still in Hunan, Guizhou and Sichuan; it was not until July 1936 that the rest two armies got over the Min Mountains.

念 奴 嬌

niàn nú jiāo

昆 侖

kūn lún

横空出世。

héng kōng chū shì

莽昆侖，

mǎng kūn lún

閲盡人間春色。

yuè jìn rén jiān chūn sè

飛起玉龍三百萬〔原注〕，

fēi qǐ yù lóng sān bǎi wàn

攬得周天寒徹。

jiǎo dé zhōu tiān hán chè

夏日消溶，

xià rì xiāo róng

江河横溢，

jiāng hé héng yì

人或為魚鱉。

rén huò wéi yú biē

千秋功罪，

qiān qiū gōng zuì

KUNLUN[1]

to the tune of Charm
of Maiden Niannu

Towering into the sky,
You, Kunlun, so vast and high,
Have kept all the spring splendeur
    of the human world in your eye!
Like three million jade dragons[*2] in flight,
You freeze the universe white.
In summer your melting snow
Making rivers[3] overflow,
Alas, men may become turtles or fish in woe. [4]
But, who ever tells us, for a time of thousand
    years long,
You, after all, have done what good or wrong?

Now let me say to Kunlun:
Too high you soar into the air,
Too much snow you bear;

誰人曾與評説？
shuí rén céng yǔ píng shuō

而今我謂昆侖：
ér jīn wǒ wèi kūn lún
不要這高，
bù yào zhè gāo
不要這多雪。
bù yào zhè duō xuě
安得倚天抽寶劍，
ān dé yǐ tiān chōu bǎo jiàn
把汝裁為三截？
bǎ rǔ cái wéi sān jié
一截遺歐，
yī jié wèi ōu
一截贈美，
yī jié zèng měi
一截還東國。
yī jié huán dōng guó
太平世界，
tài píng shì jiè
環球同此凉熱。
huán qiú tóng cǐ liáng rè

（一九三五年十月）

How, then, could I wield a heaven-high sword,
Cutting you in three to afford
One piece to Europe,
One piece to America,
And the final piece to Asia. [5]
Ah, What a peaceful world we would see,
And alike warm and cold the earth would be! [6]

(October 1935)

* AUTHOR'S ORIGINAL NOTE

An ancient poet (referring to Zhang Yuan, a scholar in the Northern Song Dynasty —— tr.) says: "The three million jade dragons end their fighting on high/Leaving behind their tattered scales whirling in the sky." The description is about the flying snow. Now I just borrow the first line to describe the snow-covered mountains. In summer, when one ascends Min Mountains to command a distant view, one finds all mountains are dancing in an expanse of whiteness. People here say all these mountains were afire when the Monkey King [7] passed through the place; it was non other than the monkey who borrowed a palm leaf fan and quenched the flames, thus the mountains all turned white.

〔原注〕前人所謂"戰罷玉龍三百萬,敗鱗殘甲滿天飛",說的是飛雪。這裏借用一句,說的是雪山。夏日登岷山遠望,群山飛舞,一片皆白。老百姓說,當年孫行者過此,都是火焰山,就是他借了芭蕉扇搧滅了火,所以變白了。

TRANSLATOR'S NOTES

1. Kunlun: mountain ranges, situated in the west of China, with its highest peak of 25348 feet above the sea level; it is on the north edge of Tibetan Plateau, extending from Pamirs and Karakoram Range into Qinghai, having many subsidiary ranges. In June 1935, the Red Army climbed over Jiajin Mountain and Min Mountain which are also the subsidiary ranges of Kunlun Mountain Ranges.

2. jade dragons: snow-covered mountains.

3. rivers: specifically referring to the Yangzi River and the Yellow River both of which originating in the subsidiary ranges of Kunlun.

4. men may become turtles or fish in woe: men may be drowned. *Commentaries on the Spring and Autumn Annals* (Zuozhuan) by Zuo Qiuming: "Without Great Yu to regulate the rivers and watercourses, we all would have become fish." *History of the Later Han Dynasty* (by Fan Ye), vol. 1: "Liu Lin persuades Liu Xiu, the Guangwu Emperor: 'The Chimei rebels now station at the east end of the river, if we breach the dam to flood them, a million strong will become fish.' " Du Fu's "The Officer at the Tongguan Pass": "Alas the battle at Taolin by the Yellow River/Made a million strong become fish. "

5. Asia: In Mao's first draft, it was "China", not "Asia". The correction was made in the 1963 edition of *Poems of Chairman Mao* (People's Literature Press, 1963).

6. The second stanza means that communism will be thus realized throughout the world.

7. the Monkey King: also called Sun Wukong, a saint-like monster who escorts a monk called Tang Sanzang to go to the west for Buddhist Cannons. Finding the Fire Mountains standing in the way, the monkey, suffering a lot of setbacks, finally succeeds in getting over the Fire Mountains with his master the monk and the other two disciples of the monk, by borrowing a palm leaf fan to quench the fire. For details, see *Pilgrimage to the West* by Wu Cheng-én (?1500-?1582).

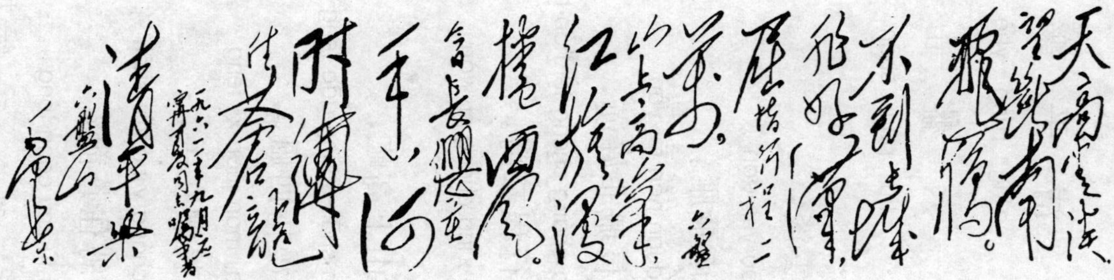

清　平　樂
qīng　píng　yuè

六　盤　山
liù　pán　shān

天高雲淡，
tiān gāo yún dàn

望斷南飛雁。
wàng duàn nán fēi yàn

不到長城非好漢，
bú dào cháng chéng fēi hǎo hàn

屈指行程二萬。
qū zhǐ xíng chéng èr wàn

六盤山上高峰，
liù pán shān shàng gāo fēng

紅旗漫捲西風。
hóng qí màn juǎn xī fēng

今日長纓在手，
jīn rì cháng yīng zài shǒu

何時縛住蒼龍？
hé shí fù zhù cāng lóng

（一九三五年十月）

MOUNT LIUPAN[1]
to the tune of Music of Peace

The skies are deep, clouds are thinly wan;
Fading into the south heaven wild geese we
scan. [2]
One is not a man if failing to reach the
Great Wall, [3]
Counting, we know we've covered twenty
thousand li in all.

High on the peak of Mount Liupan,
In the west wind red flags flap and sound.
We now hold the long cord in hand, [4]
When will the Dragon[5] be bound?

(October 1935)

TRANSLATOR'S NOTES

1. Mount Liupan: also called Longshan, a mountain situated south of Ningxia and east of Gansu with its highest peak of 9606 feet above the sea level. A path winding around the mountain leads to the top with six twists and turns, thus the mountain is called Six Twists Mountain (Liupanshan).

   On the afternoon of October 7, 1935, the vanguard of the Red Army climbed over the main peak of Mount Liupan, the last highest peak standing in the way to the destination of the Long March, northern Shaanxi. Mao Zedong wrote the piece right on top of the peak.

   This poem was first published in *Poetry* (January 1957).

2. Fading into the south heaven wild geese we scan: We scan wild geese fading into the south heaven. Wild geese are migratory birds which, in autumn, fly to the south to spend winter days while in spring they fly back to the north, so a wild goose image is a favourite with many traditional Chinese Poets who use it to suggest 1) autumn (southward wild geese); 2) spring (northward wild geese); 3) the missing of one's absent friend or dear one either in the south or in the north or in any far-away place. With Mao, the image suggests 1) autumn time; 2) missing the Second, Fourth and Sixth Red Armies still fighting in the south.

3. the Great Wall: the destination of the Long March. The actual destination of the Long March is Yenan in Northern Shaanxi,

quite near the Great Wall. The choice of the Great Wall in the poem I suppose possibly stems from an artistic conception that 1) the Great Wall is a symbol of power and strength of the Chinese people; 2) the image might spark off more traditionally poetic associations; 3) the Great Wall in the Chinese original is Changcheng (the Long Wall) that coincides with Changzheng (the Long March) partly in meaning and pronuciation, thus the greatness of the Great Wall (the Long Wall) is subtly compared to that of the Long March.

4. the long cord in hand: See note 4 to "March from Tingzhou to Changsha —— to the tune of Butterflies Love Flowers".

5. the Dragon: The original is Canglong (the Grey Dragon), traditionally symbolizing feudal rulers, here hinting at Chiang Kai-shek.

沁　園　春

qìn　yuán　chūn

雪

xuě

北國風光，

běi guó fēng guāng

千里冰封，

qiān lǐ bīng fēng

萬里雪飄。

wàn lǐ xuě piāo

望長城内外，

wàng cháng chéng nèi wài

惟餘莽莽；

wéi yú máng máng

大河上下，

dà hé shàng xià

頓失滔滔。

dùn shī tāo tāo

山舞銀蛇，

shān wǔ yín shé

SNOW[1]

to the tune of Spring
Beaming in Garden

What a scene is in the north found![2]
A thousand li of the earth is ice-clad
    aground,
Ten thousand li of the sky is snow-bound.
Behold! At both sides of the Great Wall
An expanse of whiteness conquers all;
In the Yellow River, up and down,
The surging waves are gone!
Like silver snakes the mountains dance,
Like wax elephants the highlands bounce, [*]
All try to be higher than heaven even once!
Come, when the day is fine and bright,
How you'll be enamoured of the beautiful
    sight,
To view the land adorned in red and white.

With so much beauty is the land endowed,

原馳蠟象〔原注〕，
yuán chí là xiàng

欲與天公試比高。
yù yǔ tiān gōng shì bǐ gāo

須晴日，
xū qíng rì

看紅裝素裹，
kàn hóng zhuāng sù guǒ

分外妖嬈。
fèn wài yāo ráo

江山如此多嬌，
jiāng shān rú cǐ duō jiāo

引無數英雄競折腰。
yǐn wú shù yīng xióng jìng zhé yāo

惜秦皇漢武，
xī qín huáng hàn wǔ

略輸文采；
lüè shū wén cǎi

唐宗宋祖，
táng zōng sòng zǔ

稍遜風騷。
shāo xùn fēng sāo

一代天驕，
yī dài tiān jiāo

So many heroes thus in homage bowed.

The first king of Qin[3] and the seventh king
    of Han[4],

Neither was a true literary man;

The first king of Song[5] and the second king
    of Tang,[6]

Neither was noted for poetry or song.

Even the Proud Son of Heaven, for a time,

Called Genghis Khan,[7] in his prime,

Knowing only shooting eagle, over his tent
with a bow so bent.

Alas, all no longer remain!

For truly great men,[8]

One should look within this age's ken.

(February 1936)

* **AUTHOR'S NOTE**

the highlands: here referring to loess plateau stretching
across Shanxi and Shaanxi Provinces.

成吉思汗，
chéng jí sī hán

只識彎弓射大雕。
zhǐ shí wān gōng shè dà diāo

俱往矣，
jù wǎng yǐ

數風流人物，
shǔ fēng liú rén wù

還看今朝。
hái kàn jīn zhāo

（一九三六年二月）

〔原注〕"原"指高原，即秦晉高原。

102

TRANSLATOR'S NOTES

1. Snow: When this poem was written, Mao Zedong stayed in Yuanjiagou of the Qingjian County, Shaanxi Province, planning to lead the Red Army in making an eastern journey to the Anti-Japanese War front at Hebei Province. The publication of the poem in Chongqing in 1945 caused a sentional stir in China. On August 28, 1945, Mao Zedong flew to Chongqing for a peace talk with the Kuomintang governemnt. The talk lasted 43 days during which Liu Yazi kept asking Mao for poems, Mao therefore penned the piece and gave it to him. On obtaining Mao Zedong's poem, Liu immediatly wrote a poem to the same tune as a reply and sent both Mao's and his poems to *New China Daily* for publication. *New China Daily* was then the voice of the Chinese Communist Party in Chongqing; feeling it improper to publish the poem without the permission of Mao himself, who, at the time, had already flown back to Yenan, the editor of the *Daily* published only Liu's poem on November 11, 1945; this in turn aroused more people's interest in reading Mao's original piece. At this time, a correspondent of the *New Citizen Evening Paper* happened to be in possession of the copy of the poem, the *Evening Paper* thus losed no time publishing it on December 14. On December 28, *Ta Kung Pao* republished both Mao's and Liu's poems. Kuomintang seized the chance to attack Mao for what they called Mao's ambition of assuming emperorship while communists and many other writers or scholars wrote in support of Mao.

2. What a scene is in the north found: What a scene is found in the north.

3. The first king of Qin: also called Yingzheng (259B. C. -210B. C.) in the Qin Dynasty, who conquered all the other states during the Warring States period (475 B. C. -221 B. C.) and founded the first centralized state power in China.

4. the seventh king of Han: Liu Che (156 B. C. -87 B. C.), the seventh king of the Han Dynasty (206 B. C. -220 A. D.), noted for his political and military achievements in Chinese history.

5. the first king of Song: Zhao Kuangyin (927-976), the first king of the Song Dynasty, who built out of the political and military chaos of Five Dynasties and Ten States period a united central power in China.

6. the second king of Tang: Li Shimin (599-649), the second king of the Tang Dynasty, well known for his political and military talents of helping his father, Li Yuan, to overthrow the Sui Dynasty and found the Tang Dynasty.

7. Genghis Khan: the Mongol conqueror and emperor (1162-1227), who gained control of Mongolia (1206) and conquered northern China (1211-15), then vast territories in central and southern Asia as well as Asia Minor. After his death his dominions, which stretched from the Pacific Ocean to the Black Sea, were divided among his descendants. His grandson, Kublai Khan (1260-94), completed his family's conquest of China and established his capital at Cambaluc (modern

104

Peking). He founded the Yuan Dynasty (1279-1368) and conferred a posthumous title of the First Emperor of the Yuan Dynasty upon his father, Genghis Khan.

8. truly great men: Mao gave a note to this poem on December 21, 1958, that "truly great men" refers to the proletariat.

七　律
qī　　lǜ

人民解放军佔领南京
rén mín jiě fàng jūn zhàn lǐng nán jīng

鍾山風雨起蒼黃，
zhōng shān fēng yǔ qǐ cāng huáng

百萬雄師過大江。
bǎi wàn xióng shī guò dà jiāng

虎踞龍盤今勝昔，
hǔ jù lóng pán jīn shèng xī

天翻地覆慨而慷。
tiān fān dì fù kǎi ér kāng

宜將剩勇追窮寇，
yí jiāng shèng yǒng zhuī qióng kòu

不可沽名學霸王。
bù kě gū míng xué bà wáng

天若有情天亦老，
tiān ruò yǒu qíng tiān yì lǎo

人間正道是滄桑。
rén jiān zhèng dào shì cāng sāng

(一九四九年四月)

THE PEOPLE'S LIBERATION ARMY CAPTURES NANKING[1]

to the tune of Seven-character Lü Shi

Over the Bell Mountain[2] a tremendous
  storm sweeps headlong,
Crossing the Yangzi River, our army is
  mighty, a million strong.
Once a den of tiger and dragon[3], now a
  victorious town,
How excited we are, seeing heaven and
  earth upside-down!
We now should pursue the defeated foe
  with our remaining power,[4]
Ape not King Xiang for a fame of mercy in
  a lucky hour.[5]
Were Nature sentimental, she would have
  a dying day,[6]
The change of seas into lands is Man's
  world's true way![7]

(April 1949)

107

TRANSLATOR'S NOTES

1. The People's Liberation Army Captures Nanking: Soon after the Anti-Japanese War in 1946, there broke out the Civil War between the armies under Kuomintang and those under the Chinese Communist Party. From September 1948 to January 1949, the People's Liberation Army won three smashing victories respectively in Liaoshen Battle, Huaihai Battle, and Pingjin Battle. The greater part of the land beyond the north of the Yangzi River was under the control of the People's Liberation Army. At this critical hour, peace talks were tried but in vain. On April 21, 1949, the People's Liberation Army launched a general attack upon the line of defense on the part of the Kuomintang Armies. On April 23, Nanking, the political centre of the Kuomintang government, was captured by the People's Liberation Army. At the news of the victory, Mao Zedong, wild with joy, rushed off the poem and sent it immediately to the front by telegramme in order to encourage the soldiers and civilians on the front.

   This poem was first published in the 1963 edition of *Poems of Chairman Mao* (People's Literature Press, Peking, 1963).

2. the Bell Mountain: a mountain located in the eastern suburb of Nanking, 7 kilometres in length, 3 kilometres in breadth, with the main peak of 1257 feet above the sea level. The mountain in the sunlight looks purple, thus it is also called Purple Gold Mountain (Zijinshan).

3. Once a den of tigers and dragons: a metaphor used by Zhuge Liang (a famous statesman and military strategist in the Shu State of the Three Kingdoms) to describe the meandering Bell Mountain in Nanking and the steepy Stone City in Nanking respectively as a dragon and a tiger.

4. We should pursue the defeated foe with our remaining power: typical of Mao Zedong's way of thinking against the traditional ideas. In *The Art of War by Sun Zi*, chapter VII, one finds the warning: "Pursue not the defeated foe." And Mao disagrees with Sun Zi's point of view; his disagreement stems from his intention to completely wipe out the Kuomintang forces in China. For further information, see the following notes.

5. Ape not King Xiang for a fame of mercy in a lucky hour: King Xiang, i. e. Xiang Yu (232 B. C. -202 B. C.), a leader of nobles in the Qin Dynasty. Both Xiang Yu and Liu Bang were rebel leaders who rose in arms against the Qin Dynasty. After the Qin Dynasty was overthrown, Xiang Yu was the strongest of the rebel leaders, yet, for a vain name of playing fair, he let off Liu Bang at a banquet without listening to his advisor Xiangbo's advice to kill Liu, a potential competitor of Xiang Yu for the throne. Later on, in a war between Xiang Yu and Liu Bang, Xiang got a better hand of Liu, but again, out of mercy, Xiang Yu signed a peace treaty with Liu Bang. However, soon after Xiang Yu withdrew to the east, Liu Bang, by a breach of the peace treaty, staged a surprise attack upon Xiang Yu, and finally destroyed Xiang Yu's troops.

Before the People's Liberation Army crossed the Yangzi River and captured Nanking, there were suggestions both at home and abroad that the Chinese Communist Party and the Kuomintang government could come to terms on condition that C. P. C be the master of the land north of the Yangzi River while K. M. T. be the ruler of the land south of the River. Mao flatly refused such an idea; his poem was an answer to the suggestions.

6. Were Nature sentimental, she would have a dying day: The line is quoted from Li He (790-816), a Tang poet, whose "Ode to the Golden Bronze Immortal's Taking Leave of the Han Palaces" contains such lines to the effect that on the Xianyang Road even declining orchids wave goodbye to the Golden Bronze Immortal; were Nature sentimental, she would have a dying day. The Golden Bronze Immortal was made of bronze during the reign of Hanwu Emperor, which was 219 feet tall and ten arm spans around, magnificently standing on the Divinity Platform. In 237, it was intended to be moved to Luoyang; when Weiming Emperor had it dismantled, it began to shed tears. Li He's poem is partly based on this legend.

Interpretations of Mao Zedong's message implicit in the quotation have been various. I hope the following understanding may not go wide of the mark, i. e. Mao firmly holds that the People's Liberation Army should take a merciless attitude towards the inevitable destruction of the Kuomintang regime.

7. The change of seas into lands is Man's world's true way: an allusion from Ge Hong's *Stories about Immortals*, VII, in which

110

Ma Gu says, the East Sea has been seen changed into mulberry lands three times.

七　律
qī　lù

和柳亞子先生
hè liǔ yà zǐ xiān shēng

飲茶粵海未能忘，
yǐn chá yuè hǎi wèi néng wàng

索句渝州葉正黃。
suò jù yú zhōu yè zhèng huáng

三十一年還舊國，
sān shí yī nián huán jiù guó

落花時節讀華章。
luò huā shí jié dú huá zhāng

牢騷太盛防腸斷，
láo sāo tài shèng fáng cháng duàn

風物長宜放眼量。
fēng wù cháng yí fàng yǎn liáng

莫道昆明池水淺，
mò dào kūn míng chí shuǐ qiǎn

觀魚勝過富春江。
guān yú shèng guò fù chūn jiāng

（一九四九年四月二十九日）

REPLY TO MR. LIU YAZI[1]
to the tune of Seven-Character Lü Shi

The memory of our drinking tea at
    Guangzhou is fresh still,
And you asked me for poems at Chong-
    qing as yellow leaves were chill.
I come back now in the old city after
    thirty-one years past,
I readily read your beautiful lines at the
    season when flowers blast.

Grievances, if too many, would wound
    seriously one's heart,
Weighing things one should be farsighted
    over a whole or part.
Say not too shallow here is the water of
    Kunming Lake,[2]
It is better than Fuchun River[3] to watch-
    ing fish for one to take.

                    (April 29, 1949)

TRANSLATOR'S NOTES

1. Liu Yazi: also named Wei Gao (1887-1958), Qi Ji, An Ru, Ya Lu, etc. ; a native of Wujiang, Jiangsu Province. He was a poet, an organizer, and later on, chairman of the South Society (1906) that was a literary body against the Qing Dynasty (1644-1911). In 1912, he served as secretary to Sun Yat-sen, president of the Chinese Republic. In February 1949, Mao Zedong invited Liu Yazi (then in Hong Kong) to take part in the preparation of the Chinese People's Political Consultation Conference. On March 18, Liu Yazi arrived in Peking with his wife. Seven days later on March 25, Mao Zedong, too, came back to Peking from Shijiazhuang; Liu and other democratic personages went to meet Mao at the airport. At the night, they all attended a banquet held in the Summer Palace. Three days later, however, what with certain contradictions existing in democratic parties and what with his inability to have a special car to offer a sacrifice to Sun Yat-sen's mourning hall in Biyun Temple at Xiangshan, Liu Yazi gave vent to his grievances by writing a poem on the night of March 28 and presented the poem to Mao Zedong. On reading it, Mao immediatly instructed the authority concerned to arrange well for Liu's daily life, and, on the next day, Mao wrote the poem "Reply to Mr. Liu Yazi", in which one can easily feel the note of persuasion and advice. Again, on May 1, Mao visited Liu at the Summer Palace.

   This poem was first published in *Poetry* (January 1957).

114

2. Kunming Lake: the lake in the Summer Palace, with an area of 220 hectares.

3. Fuchun River: another name of Qiantang River, flowing through the middle of Zhejiang Province. The line alludes to Yan Guang, a statesman in the Eastern Han Dynasty, who once fished with a hook and line on the bank of the Qiantang River.

附：柳亞子原詩

七　律
qī　lù

感事呈毛主席
gǎn shì chéng máo zhǔ xí

開天闢地君真健，
kāi tiān pì dì jūn zhēn jiàn

說項依劉我大難。
shuō xiàng yī liú wǒ dà nán

奪席談經非五鹿，
duó xí tán jīng fēi wǔ lù

無車彈鋏怨馮驩。
wú chē tán jiá yuàn féng huān

頭顱早悔平生賤，
tóu lú zǎo huǐ píng shēng jiàn

肝膽寧忘一寸丹！
gān dǎn nìng wàng yī cùn dān

安得南征馳捷報，
ān dé nán zhēng chí jié bào

Liu Yazi's Poem
MY THOUGHTS PRESENTED
TO CHAIRMAN MAO[1]
to the tune of Seven-Character Lü Shi

Of the new heaven and earth you are the great mak-
    er!
Canvassing between Xiang and Liu[2] I am an embar-
    rassed talker.
Not being Wulu[3] who silences scholars by an impe-
    rial support,
I am cold-shouldered Feng[4] lacking a cart to a sum-
    mer resort.
Feeling sorrow in early years for this low-priced
    head[5] of mine,
After all, deep in my heart sincerity and loyalty
    still shine.
O that from the southern expedition[6] the news of
    victory come,
Then like Zi Ling[7] by the lake of Fenhu[8] a hermit I'll
    become. *

(April 28, 1949)

117

分湖便是子陵灘。〔原注〕
fēn hú biàn shì zǐ líng tān

（一九四九年四月二十八日）

〔原注〕分湖為吳越間巨浸，元季楊鐵崖曾遊其地，因以得名。余家世居分湖之北，名大勝村。第宅為倭寇所毀。先德舊疇，思之淒絕！

Fenhu is a large lake extending beyond Jiangsu and Zhejiang Provinces. Near the end of the Yuan Dynasty, Yang Tieya (1296-1376, a noted poet and calligrapher) visited the lake, and thus the lake was later on named in connection with Yang's visit. My native place is the Dasheng Village located to the north of the lake, where my family had lived for generations, but the illustrious mansions of my old home were destroyed by Japanese invaders. Alas, whenever thinking of the renowned virtues and property handed down from my forefathers yet now reduced to ashes, I am obssessed with deep sorrows beyond compare.

TRANSLATOR'S NOTES

1. My thoughts presented to Chairman Mao: See note 1 to "Reply to Mr. Liu Yazi — to the tune of Seven-Character Lü Shi".

2. Canvassing between Xiang and Liu: persuading King Xiang to submit to King Liu. Xiang, Xiang Yu; Liu, Liu Bang; see notes to "The People's Liberation Army Captures Nanking". Here "Xiang" alludes to Chiang Kai-shek and the Nanking government; "Liu" alludes to Mao Zedong and the Chinese Communist Party. At the time Liu Yazi wrote the poem, the Chinese Communist Party was making efforts to persuade the Nanking government to accept a peace treaty, hoping other democratic personages would join in the efforts. Liu Yazi here means he is powerless in undertaking the attempt, though he is a founding member of Kuomintang.

3. Wulu: Wulu Chongzong, a scholar in the Western Han Dynasty. He was a favourite with Liu Shi, an emperor of the Han Dynasty, thus all the scholars then were afraid of disagreeing with him when he lectured on *The Book of Change*.

4. Feng: a talented figure in the State of Qi during the Warring States period. Feng Huan was a hanger-on of Meng Changjun, an aritocrat. Dissatisfied with his lowgrade status, he vent his grievances by tapping on the hilt of his sword singing, "Return, my sword! I eat without fish. " He was thus granted the middle-grade treatment; yet still dissatisfied, he sang again,

120

"Return, my sword! I walk without a cart." He was finally satisfied with a cart, treated as one of the highest-grade hangers-on. Liu Yazi here hints obliquely at his inability to secure a car to go to Sun Yat-sen's mourning hall at Xiangshan. See note 1 to Mao's "Reply to Mr. Liu Yazi".

5. low-priced head: Chiang Kai-shek once offered a reward to arrest Liu Yazi, but the reward was not of the highest price.

6. the southern expedition: the People's Liberation Army's punitive expedition against Chiang Kai-shek regime in the south (Nanking).

7. Zi Ling: also named Yan Guang, a renowned scholar in the Eastern Han Dynasty. He was a good friend of Liu Xiu, an emperor of the Eastern Han Dynasty. Instead of accepting Liu Xiu's offer to be a high official, he returned to his native place, tilling the land and fishing by the Qili Lake.

8. the lake of Fenhu: a lake located in the south of the Wujiang County, Jiangsu Province, here standing for Liu Yazi's native place.

浣 溪 沙
huàn xī shā

和柳亞子先生
hè liǔ yà zǐ xiān shēng

一九五〇年國慶觀劇,柳亞子先生即席賦《浣溪沙》,因步其韻奉和。

長夜難明赤縣天,
cháng yè nán míng chì xiàn tiān

百年魔怪舞翩躚,
bǎi nián mó guài wǔ piān xiān

人民五億不團圓。
rén mín wǔ yì bù tuán yuán

一唱雄鷄天下白,
yī chàng xióng jī tiān xià bái

萬方樂奏有于闐,
wàn fāng yuè zòu yǒu yú tián

詩人興會更無前。
shī rén xìng huì gèng wú qián

(一九五〇年十月)

REPLY TO MR. LIU YAZI[1]
to the tune of
Silk-Washing Stream

In celebration of the National Day, 1950, Mr. Liu Yazi composed a poem impromptu to the tune of Silk-Washing Stream at a song and dance performance, to which I replied, employing the same rhyme pattern.

The long night long enshrouded the sky
    over the Red State,[2]
For a century[3] devils and monsters[4] danced
    in an ugly gait,
And five hundred million people[5] suffered a
    split-up fate.

At a crow of the cock the dark world is sud-
    denly exposed to light![6]
Glad music comes from all corners[7], even
    Yutian[8], the remotest site.
Never before has the zeal of the poet[9] been
    inspired to such a height!

(October 1950)

123

TRANSLATOR'S NOTES

1. Reply to Mr. Liu Yazi: On the evening of October 3, 1950, in watching a song and dance performance in celebration of the National Day, Mr. Liu Yazi sat in the row right before Mao Zedong's seat; Mao said cheerfully to Liu, "On such a grand occassion, what about composing a ci-poetry in memory of it? I will reply to your composition." Liu immediately improvised a ci-poetry to the tune of Silk-washing Stream and presented it to Mao Zedong. The next day, Mao wrote "Reply to Mr. Liu Yazi" to the same tune.

   This poem was first published in *Poetry* (January 1957).

2. the Red State: China. The name was first used by Zou Yan, a scholar in the period of Warring States.

3. For a century: for a hundred years from 1840 (the Opium War) to 1950 (the founding of the People's Republic of China).

4. devils and monsters: imperialists and feudalists.

5. five hundred million people: in 1950, China's population amounted to about four hundred and fifty million.

6. At a crow of the cock the dark world is suddenly exposed to light: The line is quoted with a slight change from Li He (790-816), a poet in the Tang Dynasty.

7. all corners: throughout the country.

8. Yutian: a county in the Xinjiang Uygur (Uighur) Au-

tonomous Region.

9. the poet: 1) poets in general; 2) specifically referring to Liu
Yazi and Mao Zedong himself.

附：柳亞子原詞

浣 溪 沙
huàn xī shā

十月三日之夕于懷仁堂觀西南各民族文工團、新疆文工團、吉林省延邊文工團、內蒙文工團聯合演出歌舞晚會,毛主席命填是闋,用紀大團結之盛況云爾!

火樹銀花不夜天。
huǒ shù yín huā bú yè tiān

弟兄姊妹舞翩躚。
dì xiōng zǐ mèi wǔ piān xiān

歌聲唱徹月兒圓。〔原注〕
gē shēng chàng chè yuè ér yuán

不是一人能領導,
bù shì yī rén néng lǐng dǎo

那容百族共駢闐?
nà róng bǎi zú gòng pián tián

良宵盛會喜空前!
liáng xiāo shèng huì xǐ kōng qián

(一九五〇年十月三日)

〔原注〕新疆哈薩克族民間歌舞有《圓月》一歌云。

126

Liu Yazi's Poem

to the tune of Silk-Washing Stream

On the evening of October 3, I attended a soirée in Huairen Hall. The joint performances were given by song and dance ensembles from the various nationalities in the Southwest, Xinjiang, Yanbian in Jilin Province, and Inner Mongolia. At Chairman Mao's request, I composed the following poem to celebrate the great unity of the nationalities.

With fiery trees and silvery flowers it is a darkless
    night,
Brothers and sisters dance gracefully all with their
    feet light.
Songs echo The Full Moon* through so far and so
    wide.

But for one man who has offered his brilliant and
    wise guide,
How could today the hundred peoples fortunately
    assemble here?
Never before have we enjoyed a grand gathering

127

with good cheer.

(October 3, 1950)

* Liu Yazi's note:

There is a Kazakh folk song in Xinjiang called The Full
Moon.

浪淘沙　北戴河

大雨落幽燕，白浪滔天，秦皇岛外打鱼船。一片汪洋都不见，知向谁边？

往事越千年，魏武挥鞭，东临碣石有遗篇。萧瑟秋风今又是，换了人间。

浪 淘 沙
làng táo shā

北 戴 河
běi dài hé

大雨落幽燕，
dà yǔ luò yōu yān

白浪滔天，
bái làng tāo tiān

秦皇島外打魚船。
qín huáng dǎo wài dǎ yú chuán

一片汪洋都不見，
yī piàn wāng yáng dōu bú jiàn

知向誰邊？
zhī xiàng shuí biān

往事越千年，
wǎng shì yuè qiān nián

魏武揮鞭，
wèi wǔ huī biān

BEIDAIHE[1]
to the tune of Waves Sift Sand

The northern land is bathed in a torrential
    rain,
Whitecaps in the Bohai Sea leap to the star-
    high domain,
While far beyond Qinhuangdao[2] the fishing
    boat
Is not seen on the boundless main,
Where does it float?

Two thousand years ago just on this land,
The Emperor Weiwu,[3] whip in hand,
Rode eastward to Jieshi,[4] his poems of the
    autumnal sea remain;
Now the autumn wind sighs again,
But the old world has changed its reign.

(Summer 1954)

東臨碣石有遺篇。
dōng lín jié shí yǒu yí piān

蕭瑟秋風今又是
xiāo sè qiū fēng jīn yòu shì

換了人間。
huàn le rén jiān

（一九五四年夏）

TRANSLATOR'S NOTES

1. Beidaihe: a famous scenic spot, located in the southwest of Qinhuangdao, Hebei Province, opened up as a summer resort even in 1898. In the summer of 1954, Mao Zedong was there spending his holiday. One day, there arose on the sea a storm and the surging waves splashed the shore. Mao wanted to swim in the sea but he was rebuffed by his guards; Mao insisted and succeeded in swimming in the sea for over one hour. The poem was written after Mao finished swimming.

    This poem was first published in *Poetry* (January 1957).

2. Qinhuangdao: the Qin Emperor Island, located in the east of Hebei Province, a peninsula in crescent shape. Qin Shi Huang, the First Emperor of the Qin Dynasty (221 B. C. -207 B. C.), was said to have stayed there for a time seeking immortals; hence the name.

3. The Emperor Weiwu: Cao Cao (155-220), a noted statesman, military strategist and poet in the period of the Three Kingdoms. Cao Cao was the founder of the State of Wei; after his son, Cao Pi(187-226), ascended the throne, he was conferred on the posthumous title of Emperor Weiwu.

4. Jieshi: 1) a mountain situated in the Changli County, Hebei Province; 2) a mountain situated in the Suizhong County, Liaoning Province, 15 kilometres from the Shanhai Pass (the Mountain-and-Sea Pass). In the autumn of 207, Cao Cao con-

133

quered the tribe called Wuhuan in the north, while on his way back, he passed by Jieshi Mountain, and there he wrote a few poems, of which "A View of the Great Sea" is referred to in Mao Zedong's poem:

A View of the Great Sea

I come eastward to Jieshi
to scan the endless sea.
Look how waters roll,
how islands soar,
how trees thrive,
how grasses lushly grow.
The wind howls and sighs;
The billowy breakers leap,
The sun and the moon
seem to journey through waves;
The stars and the Milky Way
seem to gleam in the foams.
How great is my delight!
I chant it in this song.

水 調 歌 頭
shuǐ diào gē tóu

游　　泳
yóu　　yǒng

才飲長沙水，
cái yǐn cháng shā shuǐ

又食武昌魚。
yòu shí wǔ chāng yú

萬里長江橫渡，
wàn lǐ cháng jiāng héng dù

極目楚天舒。
jí mù chǔ tiān shū

不管風吹浪打，
bù guǎn fēng chuī làng dǎ

勝似閒庭信步，
shèng sì xián tíng xìn bù

今日得寬餘。
jīn rì dé kuān yú

子在川上曰：
zǐ zài chuāng shàng yuē

SWIMMING[1]

to the tune of Prelude
to Water Melody

The waters of Changsha[2] just drunk is a
    good brew,
Now I come to taste the Wuchang fish[3]
    stew;
Swimming across the longest Yangzi Riv-
    er,
Looking as far as my eye can reach to the
    sky of Chu. [4]
Let the wind blow and waves swill,
To me, its better than having a stroll
In a courtyard at will.
Ah, today, how much at ease I feel.
"By the river Confucius[5] is heard to say:
Thus do things flow away!"[6]

Lo! Sails move with the wind,

逝者如斯夫！
shì zhě rú sī fū

風檣動，
fēng qiáng dòng

龜蛇静，
guī shé jìng

起宏圖。
qǐ hóng tú

一橋飛架南北，
yī qiáo fēi jià nán běi

天塹變通途。
tiān qiàn biàn tōng tú

更立西江石壁，
gèng lì xī jiāng shí bì

截斷巫山雲雨，
jié duàn wū shān yún yǔ

高峽出平湖。
gāo xiá chū píng hú

神女應無恙，
shén nǚ yīng wú yàng

當驚世界殊。
dāng jīng shì jiè shū

（一九五六年六月）

138

Tortoise and Snake[7] silently stand,

We begin a plan so grand ——

To span the north and south a bridge we
will lay,

The chasm will be turned into a broad
high-way.

A dam will be built across the upstream to
the west,

Bringing Wushan Mountains'[8] clouds and
rain to rest,

A lake will appear around the deep gorge's
crest.

Should the Wushan goddess be alive and
sound today,

She would marvel at the world now in new
array.

(June 1956)

TRANSLATOR'S NOTES

1. Swimming: In 1956, Mao Zedong made an inspection tour of various places throughout China; at the end of May of the year, he came to Wuhan, where he swam in the Yangzi River three times respectively on June 1, 3 and 4. What is written in the poem above is about his first swimming.

   This poem was first published in *Poetry* (June 1957).

2. The waters of Changsha: On December 21, 1958, Mao Zedong made a note to the line: "What is called the waters of Changsha is found in the eastern city of Changsha where locates a well-known well named 'The White Sand Well'".

3. Wuchang fish: a sort of round-head bream, tasting delicious, a specialty well-known in Fankou of the Ezhou County, Hubei Province. These two lines mean "I have just been to Changsha, and now I am in Wuhan again." The allusion is from a children's folk rhyme current in the period of the Three Kingdoms (220-280): "We would rather drink waters of Jianye (now the city of Nanking) than eat Wuchang fish", because people then were against Sun Hao, the ruler of Wu, for his idea of moving the capital of the State of Wu from Jianye to Wuchang (now the Ezhou County). But here in Mao's poem, Wuchang refers to one of the three cities of Wuhan.

4. Swimming across ... to the sky of Chu: In a letter to Huang Yanpei, dated February 11, 1957, Mao Zedong says, "When I

140

swam in the Yangzi River, I spent two hours drifting on the waters for more than thirty li to reach the opposite bank; the waters was indeed swift. I kept relying on backstrokes and side strokes; it is, therefore, appropriate for me to describe the situation as 'Looking as far as my eye can reach to the sky of Chu'".

5. Confucius: Kong Qiu (551 B. C. -449 B. C.), the famous scholar, thinker, statesman, educator as well as the originator of Confucianism, in China.

6. Thus do things flow away: These two lines are quoted from *The Analects of Confucius*: "Standing by a river, the master says, things do flow away like this without stopping, day or night." (*The Analects of Confucius*, chapter Zi Han, 9. 17).

7. Tortoise and Snake: the names of the two mountains. The Tortoise Mountain shaping like a tortoise is situated north of Hanyang, one of the three cities of Wuhan; while the Snake Mountain shaping like a snake threads through the city of Wuchang.

8. Wushan Mountains: mountains situated in the east of the Wushan County, Sichuan Province, with twelve peaks in all, six in the north, six in the south.

蝶 戀 花

dié liàn huā

答李淑一

dá lǐ shū yī

我失驕楊君失柳，

wǒ shī jiāo yáng jūn shī liǔ

楊柳輕颺直上重霄九。

yáng liǔ qīng yáng zhí shàng chóng xiāo jiǔ

問訊吳剛何所有，

wèn xùn wú gāng hé suǒ yǒu

吳剛捧出桂花酒。

wú gāng pěng chū guì huā jiǔ

寂寞嫦娥舒廣袖，

jì mò cháng é shū guǎng xiù

萬里長空且為忠魂舞。

wàn lǐ cháng kōng qiě wéi zhōng hún wǔ

忽報人間曾伏虎，

hū bào rén jiān céng fú hǔ

淚飛頓作傾盆雨。

lèi fēi dùn zuò qīng pén yǔ

（一九五七年五月十一日）

REPLY TO LI SHUYI[1]
to the tune of Butterflies Love Flowers

You lost your darling Willow[2] and I my
    Poplar proud,[3]
Both Poplar and Willow soar gracefully
    farabove the cloud.
They ask Wu Gang[4] about what he has
    there,
It's the laurel wine[5] that Wu offers them to
    share.

The lonely goddess of the moon[6] spreads
    her sleeves long,
To console the loyal souls she dances in
    sky with a song.
Suddenly the news about the tiger sub-
    dued[7] comes from the earth,
At once the rain pours down from our
    darlings' tears of mirth.

(May 11, 1957)

TRANSLATOR'S NOTES

1. Reply to Li Shuyi: Li Shuyi (1901-   ), a native of Changsha,
   teacher of Chinese in No. 10 Middle School of Changsha. In
   1920's, Li Shuyi was a classmate as well as a good friend of
   Yang Kaihui, Mao's first wife. In 1924, through Yang
   Kaihui's introduction, Li Shuyi got to know, and later on married, Liu Zhixun (1898-1932); Liu was then one of Mao's
   comrades-in-arms. In the summer of 1933, word came that
   Liu was killed in a battle that took place in Hubei Province.
   Weighed down with sadness, Li Shuyi could not eat or sleep
   well; she later on wrote a ci-poem to the tune of Buddhist
   Dancers in memory of her husband. It was not until the founding of the People's Republic of China that Li acquired the exact
   information about the death of her husband. On January 17,
   1950, Li Shuyi wrote to Mao Zedong telling him how his wife,
   Yang Kaihui, died, and Mao replied to her on April 18. In
   January 1957, Mao Zedong's poems (18 in all) were published
   in the first issue of the magazine *Poetry* in Peking; this re-
   minded Li Shuyi of a ci-poem to the tune of The Fair Lady Yu
   that Mao Zedong wrote to Yang Kaihui when he and Yang
   were first in love many years ago. However, Li could remember only the first two lines, she thus wrote to Mao Zedong for
   the whole piece, and in passing, enclosing in the letter her
   own "Buddhist Dancers" in memory of her husband, on February 7. On May 11, Mao Zedong replied, "the poem Kaihui

told you is not fine enough to be rewritten; here is enclosed a ci-poem 'Immortals' to you. This sort of poetry is different from ancient poems about immortals, i. e. the poet himself does not appear in the poem. But in ci-poetry, a poet can describe himself, such as the ci-poems about the seventh evening of the seventh moon (according to a Chinese legend, on that evening, the Cowherd and the Weaver Maid have a rendezvous on the magpie-made bridge over the Milky Way —— tr.)". The poem Mao mentioned in the letter is the poem above.

Mao Zedong's letter and the poem to Li Shuyi was revealed to some third-year students of the Chinese Department of Hunan Normal College at their request; those students were then performing teaching practice in No. 10 Middle School of Changsha. Soon, a few students sent a copy of Mao's poem to Mao Zedong himself and asked Mao for a permission to publish the poem in their college Journal, i. e. *Journal of Hunan Normal College*. On November 25, Mao Zedong replied that the poem could be published on condition that the original title "Immortals" be changed into "To Li Shuyi" and that the errors caused by copying be corrected. Thus, the New Year's Day of 1958 saw the publication of the poem in *Journal of Hunan Normal College* (January 1958) and the reappearance of the poem in the subsequent issues of various magazines, journals and newspapers throughout China. In the 1963 edtion of *Poems of Chairman Mao* (People's Literature Press, Peking, 1963), the title "To Li Shuyi" was changed into "Reply to Li Shuyi" as it is.

2. your darling Willow: Li Shuyi's husband, Liu Zhixun. In Chinese, Willow is pronounced as [liu], the same as the pronunciation of the family name Liu. The subtlety here is that Willow (Liu) can also suggest willow catkin just as Poplar (Yang) can suggest poplar flowers; and we know the word Poplar(Yang) indicates the family name of Mao's wife, Yang Kaihui. Poplar and Yang in Chinese are the same both in sound and meaning. Thus we feel no difficult to understand the second line "Both Poplar and Willow soar gracefully far above the cloud"; it suggests the souls of Yang Kaihui and Liu Zhixun fly above the cloud to the moon like wafting willow catkins and poplar flowers.

3. My Poplar proud: My proud Poplar; Mao's wife Yang Kaihui (1901-1930). See note above and note 1 to "To Yang Kaihui —— to the tune of Congratulating Bridegroom".

4. Wu Gang: According to a Chinese tale, there is a Laurel tree as high as more than one thousand metres in the moon, and a man called Wu Gang is made to cut the tree all the year round due to his wrong doing committed when he cultivates himself to be an immortal. The tree, however, withstanding constant chopping, can never be cut down, thus Wu Gang is punished to do the job forever.

5. the laurel wine: sources unclear, possibly stemming from Mao's own reasoning: since there is laurel, there is, naturally, laurel wine.

146

6. The lonely goddess of the moon: According to the Chinese tale, the goddess of the moon is called Chang E, the wife of an ancient hero, Yi. When Yi comes into possession of an elixir vitae one day, Chang E steals and eats it, flying up to the moon and being a goddess there.

7. the tiger subdued: the Kuomintang regime was overthrown.

菩薩蠻

pú sà mán

驚　夢

jīng mèng

蘭閨索寞翻身早，

lán guī suǒ mò fān shēn zǎo

夜來觸動離愁了。

yè lái chù dòng lí chóu liǎo

底事太難堪，

dǐ shì tài nán kān

驚儂曉夢殘。

jīng nóng xiǎo mèng cán

征人何處覓？

zhēng rén hé chù mì

六載無消息，

liù zǎi wú xiāo xī

醒憶別伊時，

xǐng yì bié yī shí

滿衫清淚滋。

mǎn shān qīng lèi zī

（一九三三年夏）

148

Li Shuyi's Poem
A BROKEN DREAM
to the tune of Buddhist Dancers

Tossing about in this lonely orchid-decorated bower,
I suddenly feel the touch of parting griefs so sour.
What is that that's so unbearable for me to allay,
Breaking my lingering dream early at the break of day?

Now tell me, where is my man who has gone to war?
For six autumns from him I have heard no more.
Awakening to recall how he has been away for years,
I've found my sleeves are soaked with bitter tears.

(Summer 1933)

七律二首

qī lǜ èr shǒu

送瘟神

sòng wēn shén

讀六月三十日《人民日報》，餘江縣消滅了血吸蟲。浮想聯翩，夜不能寐。微風拂煦，旭日臨窗。遙望南天，欣然命筆。

綠水青山枉自多，

lù shuǐ qīng shān wǎng zì duō

華佗無奈小蟲何！

huá tuó wú nài xiǎo chóng hé

千村薜荔人遺矢，

qiān cūn bì lì rén yí shǐ

萬户蕭疏鬼唱歌。

wàn hù xiāo shū guǐ chàng gē

坐地日行八萬里，

zuò dì rì xíng bā wàn lǐ

巡天遙看一千河。

xún tiān yáo kàn yī qiān hé

牛郎欲問瘟神事，

niú láng yù wèn wēn shén shì

FAREWELL TO THE
GOD OF PLAGUE[1]
to the tune of Lü Shi (two poems)

*After reading through the People's Daily of June 30,
1958, which said in Yujiang County[2] schistosomiasis[3] had been
completely wiped out, I could not sleep well at night with
thoughts thronging my mind. Then in the next morning as
sunlight penetrates into my window, amid the warm breeze,
I, looking into the distant sky, pen the following lines with
great pleasure.*

1

What's the use of so many green and blue
    streams and hills,
When even Hua Tuo[4] could do nothing
    about this tiny creature of ills[5]?
Thousands of villages choked with weeds,
    men were sick in despair,
Ten thousand homes deserted; ghosts

一樣悲歡逐逝波。

yī yàng bēi huān zhú shì bō

其二

qī èr

春風楊柳萬千條，

chūn fēng yáng liǔ wàn qiān tiáo

六億神州盡舜堯。

liù yì shén zhōu jìn shùn yáo

紅雨隨心翻作浪，

hóng yǔ suí xīn fān zuò làng

青山着意化為橋。

qīng shān zhuó yì huà wéi qiáo

天連五嶺銀鋤落，

tiān lián wǔ lǐng yín chú luò

地動三河鐵臂搖。

dì dòng sān hé tiě bì yáo

借問瘟君欲何往，

jiè wèn wēn jūn yù hé wǎng

紙船明燭照天燒。

zhǐ chuán míng zhú zhào tiān shāo

（一九五八年七月一日）

152

howled everywhere.

Sitting still on the earth is travelling eighty
    thousand li a day[6],
Touring the heaven I command a distant
    view of many a Milky Way. [7]
If, of the God of Plague, the Cowherd asks
    about the plague's crime, [8]
Say griefs and happiness all are gone with
    the passage of time.

2

The spring breeze caresses thousands of
    willow wands and boughs,
Millions of people in this Divine Land[9] are
    all Shun's and Yao's. [10]
At our will swirling into waves is red and
    flowery rain, [11]
To our taste turning into bridges is the
    green mountain chain.
Shiny hoes are wielded on the Five

Ridges[12] towering into the skies,
Iron arms[13] move, the Three Rivers[14] area
are shaking in surprise.
Now, the God of Plague, we ask, where are
you bound anon?
Burning candles and paper boats to the
sky[15] we'll get you gone.

(July 1, 1958)

TRANSLATOR'S NOTES

1. Farewell to the God of Plague: Ancient Chinese people believed there were various gods in heaven who were in charge of plagues of the human world respectively. In the Eastern Han Dynasty, people began to practise a custom of sending off the god of plague at the end of the year. This poem was first published in the *People's Daily* (October 3, 1958).

2. Yujiang County: a county in Jiangxi Province.

3. schistosomiasis: a desease prevalent in Africa and other tropical areas and once seen in the south of China, occurring in human beings and animals and caused by schistosomes infesting the blood.

4. Hua Tuo: Hua Tuo (?-208), one of the most famous doctors of ancient China. He lived in the Han Dynasty, a native of Anhui Province. He was killed by Cao Cao, Emperor Weiwu, for his disobeying to attend upon the latter.

5. this tiny creature of ills: schistosomes.

6. Sitting still on the earth is travelling eighty thousand li a day: In a letter to Zhou Shizhao, dated October 25, 1958, Mao Zedong says, "The line 'Sitting still on the earth is travelling eighty thousand li a day'···is figuratively based on the fact that the earth is 12,500 kilometres in diameter; when the distance is multiplied by the ratio of the circumference of a circle to its

diameter, π, 3. 1416, we have 40, 000 kilometers, i. e. eighty thousand li. This is the very course covered by the rotation of the earth (i. e. one day's time). To go by train, ship or bus, is called travelling; travelling needs to pay the travelling expenses. Yet, to go by the earth, one need not pay any money (i. e. needn't buy any ticket). We have travelled eighty thousand li a day, but if we ask people: Is this travel? The answer must be 'No', for, 'I am motionless'. That is really unreasonable! That is constrained by custom, handicapped by superstition. Completely phenomena of daily life, yet many people feel strange about it. "

7. Touring the heaven I command a distant view of many a Milky Way: In the same letter to Zhou Shizhao, dated October 25, 1958, Mao says, "What I mean by 'Touring the heaven' is that this solar system of ours (including the earth) is moving through the Milky Way system every day and every year. The Silver River (the Chinese way of calling Milky Way——tr.)is only a single river, but rivers are numberless... We human beings are only 'touring' in one river, but we can 'command a distant view of' numberless rivers from our position. "

8. Of the God of Plague, the Cowherd asks about the plague's crime: In the same letter (see note 6 and 7), Mao says, "the cowherd is a man in the Jin Dynasty (265-420)... It is natural for him to show concern for his natives by asking about the God of Plague. "

    The story of the Cowherd is well known to the Chinese

people:Once there was a weaving girl living on the east bank of the Silver River (the Milky Way). She was the daughter of the God of Heaven, labouring hard every day to weave cloud-brocade and heavenly clothing. Having pity on her, the God of Heaven married her to the Cowherd on the west bank of the Silver River. And, once married, the weaver stopped weaving; this angered the God of Heaven, who ordered her to go back to the east bank but allowed her to meet the Cowherd only once a year, i. e. July 7 of each year.

9. this Divine Land:China.

10. Shun's and Yao's:names of lengendary monarchs in ancient China, believed to be saints and wise leaders of the people.

11. red and flowery rain:1)spring rain;2)falling flowers.

12. the Five Ridges:See note 3 to "Long March", here referring to mountains and rivers in general throughout the country.

13. Iron arms:1) arms of the working people;2) arms of cranes or excavators.

14. the Three Rivers:originally referring to the Yellow River, Huai River and Luo River, but more reasonably believed to stand for all the rivers of the country.

15. Burning candles and paper boats to the sky:According to the Chinese popular custom, people often send off the God of Plague by burning candles and paper boats to the sky at the end of the year.

七　律

qī lǜ

到　韶　山

dào sháo shān

一九五九年六月二十五日到韶山。離別這個地方已有三十二周年了。

别夢依稀咒逝川，

bié mèng yī xī zhòu shì chuān

故園三十二年前。

gù yuán sān shí èr nián qián

紅旗捲起農奴戟，

hóng qí juǎn qǐ nóng nú jǐ

黑手高懸霸主鞭。

hēi shǒu gāo xuán bà zhǔ biān

為有犧牲多壯志，

wèi yǒu xī shēng duō zhuàng zhì

敢教日月換新天。

gǎn jiào rì yuè huàn xīn tiān

SHAOSHAN REVISITED[1]

to the tune of
Seven-Character Lü Shi

On June 25, 1959, I revisited Shaoshan which I left thirty-two years ago.

Thirty-two years ago was the time I left the
native place last,
The leave-taking scene faded like a dream, I
curse the vanished past.
The serfs'[2] halberds amid the red flags were
held aloft,
While the despot's black hand raised the
whip over head oft.

Sacrifice could only rouse people's fighting
spirit and an ideal high
They dare to demand the sun and moon
change their course in a new sky,

喜看稻菽千重浪，

xǐ kàn dào shū qiān chóng làng

遍地英雄下夕煙。

biàn dì yīng xióng xià xī yān

（一九五九年六月）

Now behold, the green crops ripple into
waves upon waves beyond,
The home-bound heroes are seen in the
smoky twilight all around.

(June 1959)

TRANSLATOR'S NOTES

1. Shaoshan Revisited: Shaoshan, also named Shaoshanchong, 40 kilometers away from the town of the Xiangtan County, Hunan Province, where three counties, Xiangxiang, Ningxiang and Xiangtan, meet. "Shao" means "splendid" or "beautiful" in Chinese, thus Shaoshan means "the beautiful mountain". Mao Zedong was born there on December 26, 1893. It was also there that Mao organized a peasant movement in February 1925. From January 4 to February 5, 1927, Mao spent 32 days making a on-the-spot investigation of the peasant movement going on then in five counties of Hunan Province, i. e. Xiangtan, Xiangxiang, Hengshan, Liling and Changsha. Shaoshan was the first place for Mao to choose as a focus of investigation where he spent five days from January 4 to 9. From June 25 to 27, 1959, Mao Zedong revisited Shaoshan and stayed there for three days, during which, Mao wrote the poem.

   This poem was first published in the 1963 edition of *Poems of Chairman Mao* (People's Literature Press, Peking, 1963).

2. serfs: poor peasants.

162

3. despot: Chiang Kai-shek. In a letter to Hu Qiaomu, dated September 13, 1959, Mao Zedong says, " 'Despot' refers to Chiang Kai-shek". This couplet describes the class struggle of that period while the whole piece deals with the history of thirty-two years.

七　律

qī　lù

登　盧　山

dēng lú shān

一山飛峙大江邊，

yī shān fēi zhì dà jiāng biān

躍上葱蘢四百旋。

yuè shàng cōng lóng sì bǎi xuán

冷眼向洋看世界，

lěng yǎn xiàng yáng kàn shì jiè

熱風吹雨灑江天。

rè fēng chuī yǔ sǎ jiāng tiān

雲橫九派浮黃鶴，

yún héng jiǔ pài fú huáng hè

浪下三吳起白煙。

làng xià sān wú qǐ bái yān

陶令不知何處去，

táo lìng bù zhī hé chù qù

桃花源裏可耕田？

táo huā yuán lǐ kě gēng tián

（一九五九年七月一日）

ASCENT OF LUSHAN MOUNTAIN[1]
to the tune of Seven-Character Lü Shi

Towering above the mighty river the mountain seems about to fly,

Four hundred twists[2] to wooded heights in a flash we pass by. [3]

I now glance at the world across the ocean with a cold eye,

When hot wind[4] blows raindrops onto the waters and into the sky.

Clouds sail over the nine streams[5] with the Yellow Crane[6] in flight,

Eastward billows sweep on to Three Wu area[7] amid the foam white.

Where I ask does Tao Yuanming[8] the Prefect right now dwell?

Does he in the Peach Blossom Land[9] till the fields well?

(July 1,1959)

165

TRANSLATOR'S NOTES

1. Ascent of Lushan Mountain: Lushan Mountain, a noted scenic spot, located south of the city of Jiujiang, Jiangxi Province, extending in an unbroken chain for 25 kilometers, with its summit, Hanyang Peak, of 1474 meters above the sea level. In July 1959, there on the mountain was held the extended meeting of the Political Bureau of the Central Committee of the Chinese Communist Party. Mao Zedong arrived at Lushan Mountain at the end of June, and several days later, he wrote the poem.

    Attention must be paid to the fact that the Lushan Meeting marks a peak of ultra-left tendencies on the part of the Chinese Communist Party headed by Mao Zedong. During the meeting, Peng Dehuai, the then Minister of National Defense, was severely criticised for his candid criticism of the Party's mistakes concerning the Great Leap Forward and the People's Commune. Peng was later on more cruelly persecuted by the "gang of four"; he died on November 29, 1974. Now the wrong once done to him has been righted, but the poem here by Mao, though artistically a success, seems, to a degree, still a monument to Peng's disgrace. Thus it would be better for the English-speaking readers to appreciate the poem as a poem without referring to too many political associations.

    According to Li Rui, the poem was originally preluded with the following words: "On June 29, 1959, I ascended the Lushan Mountain where I composed a poem of eight lines
166

while I looked into the distant Poyang Lake, Yangzi River, manifold peaks vying with their charms, innumerable valleys bristling and the red sun rising in the east. "

2. Four hundred twists: In 1953, there was built a winding mountain high way leading from the foot of Lushan to the Guling Town on the mountain as long as 35 kilometers, with about 400 twists on the way.

3. to the wooded heights in a flash we pass by: Mao went up the mountain by bus.

4. hot wind: the summer wind.

5. the nine streams: See the note 2 to "Yellow Crane Tower —— to the tune of Buddhist Dancers".

6. the Yellow Crane: See the same note above.

7. Three Wu area: a general reference to the area covering lower reaches of Yangzi River. But in particular, it may refers to Wuxing (now Guzhou district in Zhejiang Province), Wujun (now Suzhou district in Jiangsu Province) and Guiji (now Shaoxing district in Zhejiang Province); or, Wujun, Wuxing and Danyang (now Nanjing district in Jiangsu Province); or, Wujun, Wuxing and Yixing (now Yixing district in Jiangsu Province); or, Suzhou, Changzhou and Huzhou. In a letter to Zhong Xuekun, dated December 29, 1959, Mao Zedong says, "What I called Three Wu traditionally refer to Suzhou, the East Wu; Changzhou, the Middle Wu; and Huzhou, the West Wu. "

8. Tao Yuanming the Prefect: also named Tao Qian (365-427), a representative poet of the Wei and Jin Dynasties. He was once

167

appointed as the Prefect of the Pengze County, Jiangxi Province; but he soon resigned from his post and returned to his native place living on his own labour as a farmer. He often visited the Lushan Mountain, because it was within easy reach of his dwelling place. Some scholars guess that Tao Yuanming the Prefect alludes to Peng Dehuai, because the latter's being dismissed from his post at the Lushan Meeting in a sense resembles Tao's resigning from his prefectural position. Some argue that the guess is wrong, because the poem is believed to be written before the beginning of the Lushan Meeting.

9. The Peach Blossom Land: an allusion from Tao Yuanming's "A Story about the Peach Blossom Land", in which, Tao describes a paradise-like place where people enjoy equality and freedom, all work and live in peace and happiness. The place bears much resemblance to Thomas More's Utopia. Mao's intention of employing the allusion from the story has been unclear for a host of annotators and scholars. Many believe Mao's tone seems to suggest a mild note of criticising Tao's utopia.

飒爽英姿五尺枪

曙光初照演兵场

中华儿女多奇志

不爱红装爱武装

七绝 为女民兵题照

七　絕
qī　jué

爲女民兵題照
wèi nǚ mín bīng tí zhào

颯爽英姿五尺槍，
sà shuǎng yīng zī wǔ chǐ qiāng

曙光初照演兵場。
shǔ guāng chū zhào yǎn bīng chǎng

中華兒女多奇志，
zhōng huá ér nǚ duō qí zhì

不愛紅裝愛武裝。
bú ài hóng zhuāng ài wǔ zhuāng

（一九六一年二月）

INSCRIPTION ON A PHOTOGRAPH OF MILITIA WOMEN[1]
to the tune of Seven-Character Jüe Ju

Valiant and heroic in bearing, with rifles
   five-foot long,
They stand on the parade ground bathed in
   the morning glow.
In China how unique and lofty are the ide-
   als of the young,[2]
Who love battle array instead of gay attire
   in show.

(February 1961)

TRANSLATOR'S NOTES

1. The poem was first published in the 1963 edition of *Poems of Chairman Mao* (People's Literature Press, Peking, 1963).
2. the young: militia women.

七　律
qī lù

答　友　人
dá yǒu rén

九嶷山上白雲飛，
jiǔ yí shān shàng bái yún fēi

帝子乘風下翠微。
dì zǐ chéng fēng xià cuì wēi

斑竹一枝千滴淚，
bān zhú yī zhī qiān dī lèi

紅霞萬朵百重衣。
hóng xiá wàn duǒ bǎi chóng yī

洞庭波湧連天雪，
dòng tíng bō yǒng lián tiān xuě

長島人歌動地詩。
cháng dǎo rén gē dòng dì shī

我欲因之夢寥廓，
wǒ yù yīn zhī mèng liáo kuò

芙蓉國裹盡朝暉。
fú róng guó lǐ jìn zhāo huī

（一九六一年）

REPLY TO A FRIEND[1]

to the tune of
Seven-Character Lü Shi

Over the Nine Puzzles Mountain[2] white
  clouds fly,
With the wind the Princesses[3] descend the
  green hills on high.
One bamboo-shoot speckled with a thousand drops of their tears,[4]
Ten thousand red clouds[5] are their robes in
  hundred tiers.[5]
Surging into the sky are snow-capped
  waves on Dongting Lake,[6]
The man[7] on the Long Islet[8] chants the poem making the earth shake.
Thereby my dream of an immense universe
  romantically begun,
I see a land of lotuses[9] illuminated bright by
  the morning sun.

(1961)

173

TRANSLATOR'S NOTES

1. A friend: referring to Zhou Shizhao(1897-1976), a native of the Ningxiang County, Hunan Province, classmate of Mao Zedong in the No. 1 Normal School of Hunan Province in early years. After the founding of the People's Republic of China, Zhou Shizhao was appointed president of the above mentioned school as well as deputy governor of the Education Department of Hunan Province. Since July, 1958, Zhou was designated as the deputy governor of Hunan Province. Mao and Zhou keptup correspondence for many years.

   This poem was first published in the 1963 edition of *Poems of Chairman Mao* (People's Literature Press, Peking, 1963).

2. the Nine Puzzles Mountain: a branch of the Mengzhu Ridge, one of the Five Ridges, situated south of the Ningyuan County, Hunan Province; with its nine peaks soaring in the same direction, the mountain indeed puzzles travellers; hence the name.

3. the Princesses: referring to E Huang and Nü Ying, the two concubines of Shun, and daughters of Yao; both Shun and Yao were legendary monarches in ancient China. Of the nine peaks, the fourth is called the E Huang Peak; the sixth, the Nü Ying Peak.

4. One bamboo-shoot speckled with a thousand drops of their

   174

tears:an allusion from a story that at the death of Shun,the two concubines wept so sadly that their tears speckled the bamboo-shoots. (See Zhang Hua,*The Records of Natural Sciences*,Vol. 8.)

5. red clouds:The original in Chinese is Hong Xia. Here,among other implications, the imagery possibly alludes to Mao Zedong's first wife,Yang Kaihui,whose childhood name was Xia Gu. The word "Xia" often means colourful clouds shining in the morning sun or in the setting sun.

6. Dongting Lake:the second largest lake in China,with an area of 2,820 square kilometres,located in the north of Hunan.

7. The man:believed to refer to Zhou Shizhao and his fellows who wrote many poems in praise of what they called socialist revolution and socialist construction at that time,not without exaggeration. (See *Appreciation of Poems by Mao Zedong*, Jiangsu Classical Books Press,1990,p. 140.)

8. the Long Islet:the Orange Island(see note 2 to "Changsha—to the tune of Spring Beaming in Garden"; here standing for Changsha.

9. a land of lotuses:Hunan Province;Hunan is said to be noted for its lotuses seen everywhere in the province.

七 絶
qī jué

爲李進同志題所攝廬山仙人洞照
wèi lǐ jìn tóng zhì tí suǒ shè lú shān xiān rén dòng zhào

暮色蒼茫看勁松，
mù sè cāng máng kàn jìng sōng

亂雲飛渡仍從容。
luàn yún fēi dù réng cóng róng

天生一個仙人洞，
tiān shēng yī gè xiān rén dòng

無限風光在險峰。
wú xiàn fēng guāng zài xiǎn fēng

（一九六一年九月九日）

176

THE IMMORTALS' CAVE[1]
INSCRIPTION ON A PHOTO TAKEN
BY COMRADE LI JIN[2]

to the tune of Seven-
Character Jue Ju

Lo ! Standing in the dusky evening these
   pines sturdy keep,[3]
So calm and quiet, withstanding billowy
   clouds[4] that past sweep.
It is nature that chisles a cave for immortals antique,
The unmatched beauty dwells on the lofty
   and perilous peak.

(September 9,1961)

TRANSLATOR'S NOTES

1. The Immortals' Cave: a natural cave, 10 metres deep, 1049 metres above the sea level, situated at the Buddha's Hand Rock in the west of the Guling Ridge of the Lushan Mountain. It is said that Lü Dongbin, an immortal in the Tang Dynasty once cultivated himself here; hence the the name of the cave.

   This poem was first published in the 1963 editon of *Poems of Chairman Mao* (People's Literature Press, Peking, 1963).

2. Li Jin: Jiang Qing (1916-1991), a native of Zhucheng, Shandong Province. Jiang was a film and theatrical actress in Shanghai in 1930's; during the Anti-Japanese War, she went to Yenan, and there she got married with Mao Zedong. Soon after Mao's death, she was arrested in October 1977, as one of the "gang of four"; she died on March 5, 1991.

3. these pines sturdy keep: these pines keep sturdy; pines, believed to stand for the Chinese Communist Party; but the original 'song' (pine) can be also understood as in the single form, thus it may refer to a single person, for example, Mao himself.

4. billowy clouds: a sad plight in which the Chinese Communist Party stayed from 1959 to 1961 when China's national economy suffered heavy setbacks and meanwhile idealogical polemics between the Chinese Communist Party and the Soviet Communist Party were bitterly engaged.

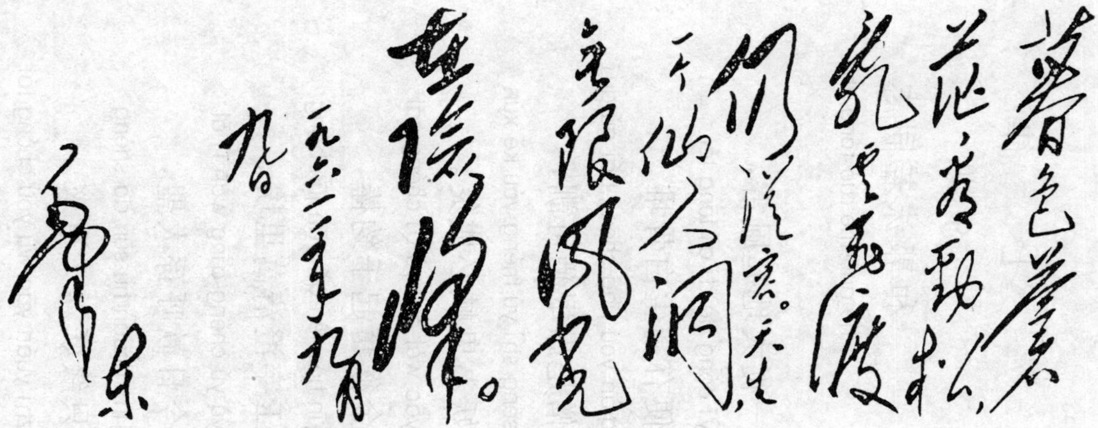

七　律

qī　lù

和郭沫若同志

hè guō mò ruò tóng zhì

一從大地起風雷，

yī cóng dà dì qǐ fēng léi

便有精生白骨堆。

biàn yǒu jīng shēng bái gǔ duī

僧是愚氓猶可訓，

sēng shì yú méng yóu kě xùn

妖為鬼蜮必成災。

yāo wéi guǐ yù bì chéng zāi

金猴奮起千鈞棒，

jīn hóu fèn qǐ qiān jūn bàng

玉宇澄清萬里埃。

yù yǔ chéng qīng wàn lǐ āi

今日歡呼孫大聖，

jīn rì huān hū sūn dà shèng

只緣妖霧又重來。

zhǐ yuán yāo wù yòu chóng lái

（一九六一年十一月十七日）

REPLY TO COMRADE GUO MORUO[1]

to the tune of Seven-Character LüShi

Ever since a thunder and storm crashes the
earth with might,

An evil demon has been born of a heap of
bones white. [2]

The monk though simple-headed is not an
uneducated moke, [3]

The demon so evil and malignant must disasters provoke.

Once the Golden Monkey wields his cudgel
of ten thousand jin,

The fair and boundless sky is soon cleared
of dust and din.

We hail Sun Dasheng, the Wonder-worker,
today,

Because the evil mist[4] rises again on the
way.

(November 17, 1961)

TRANSLATOR'S NOTES

1. Guo Moruo: Guo Kaizhen (1892-1978), alias Guo Moruo, Mai Ke-ang, Yi Kanren, Shi Tuo, Gao Ruhong, Gu Ren, Yang Yizhi, etc. , a native of Leshan, Sichuan Province. Guo is well known for his studies in ancient inscriptions on tortoise shell, ox bones and ancient tripods. He is considered a versatile scholar whose poetry writing, play writing and translation are also worthwhile to be mentioned. In early October, 1961, Mao Zedong saw a play entitled *The Golden Monkey Subdues the White Bone Demon Three Times*, which Guo Moruo also saw on October 18. On October 25, Guo wrote a seven-character Lü Shi about the play at the request of the drama group. Mao read the poem; feeling unable to agree with Guo's point of view embodied in the poem, he wrote the above poem to the same tune answering Guo's on November 17. It was on January 6, 1962, when Guo stayed in Guangzhou that Mao's poem reached Guo's hand (through a copy by Kang Sheng); Guo sensed the mild criticism suggested in the poem and he immediately replied Mao's poem to the same tune on the same day. His reply was forwarded to Mao through Kang Sheng and Mao answered, "Your reply is good. Say not 'The monk deserves to be torn limb from limb a thousand times' again. A united front policy is assumed towards the middle-of-the-roaders. That's fine."

2. Ever since... a heap of bones white: The play *The Golden Monkey Subdues the White Bone Demon Three Times* is based on Chapter 31 of *Pilgrimage to the West* by Wu Cheng-en (1500?-1582?),a noted novelist and scholar in the Ming Dynasty. According to Wu Cheng-en's story,an evil demon is born of a heap of white bones which has been absorbing the spiritual essence between the earth and heaven. Gradually it has taken the shape of a human being. To eat Tangseng,the monk from the Tang Empire,the demon assumes different human forms three times, yet three times, Sun Dasheng, the Wonder-worker, a disciple of Tangseng, sees through the tricks of the evil demon. Being unable to tell a demon from human beings,the monk reprimands Sun Dasheng for killing the human-being-like demon,thus he drives the monkey away. But Dasheng,later on,is witty enough to change himself into the form of the demon's mother to deceive and finally destroy the demon.

3. The monk ... is not an uneducated moke: It is just here that Mao Zedong does not see eye to eye with Guo Moruo. Guo regards the monk an out-and-out bad egg who should "be torn limb from limb a thousand times",while Mao thinks the monk is one who needs to be educated and won over in stead of being punished mercilessly.

4. the evil mist: mainly referring to Soviet revisionists.

七　律
qī　lǜ

看《孫悟空三打白骨精》
kàn sūn wù kōng sān dǎ bái gǔ jīng

人妖顛倒是非淆，
rén yāo diān dǎo shì fēi xiáo

對敵慈悲對友刁。
duì dí cí bēi duì yǒu diāo

咒念金箍聞萬遍，
zhòu niàn jīn gū wén wàn biàn

精逃白骨累三遭。
jīng táo bái gǔ lěi sān zāo

千刀當剮唐僧肉，
qiān dāo dāng guǎ táng sēng ròu

一拔何虧大聖毛。
yī bá hé kuī dà shèng máo

教育及時堪贊賞，
jiào yù jí shí kān zàn shǎng

豬猶智慧勝愚曹。
zhū yóu zhì huì shèng yú cáo

（一九六一年十月十八日）

Guo Moruo's Poem
THOUGHTS ON SEEING THE GOLDEN
MONKEY SUBDUES THE DEMON
THREE TIMES

Humans and demons, right and wrong, he all
blends,
The monk pities the foes and cruel to his friends.
He keeps mumbling the curse on the monkey in a
vexed tone,
And three times he let off the evil demon of white
bone.

The monk should die a thousand times if dealt
with fair,
Thanks to the monkey who comes to help by
plucking his hair.
Timely teaching proves to be a laudable and
worthy school,
So even the Pig can be taught therein wiser than a
fool.

(October 18,1961)

卜算子

bǔ suàn zǐ

詠　梅

yǒng méi

讀陸游《詠梅》詞，反其意而用之。

風雨送春歸，
fēng yǔ sòng chūn guī

飛雪迎春到。
fēi xuě yíng chūn dào

已是懸崖百丈冰，
yǐ shì xuán yá bǎi zhàng bīng

猶有花枝俏。
yóu yǒu huā zhī qiào

俏也不爭春，
qiào yě bù zhēng chūn

只把春來報。
zhǐ bǎ chūn lái bào

待到山花爛漫時，
dài dào shān huā làn màn shí

她在叢中笑。
tā zài cóng zhōng xiào

（一九六一年十二月）

186

ODE TO THE PLUM BLOSSOM[1]

to the tune of Song of Divination

After reading Lu You's "Ode to the Plum Blossom,"[2] I composed the following to the same tune yet opposite to Lu You's in theme.

Wind and rain escorted Spring to go,[3]
Now spring returns welcomed by flying
   snow.[4]
High on the cliffs are icicles[5] hundred-foot
   long, there,
A flower springs up so fair.

So fair she is, yet, not so vain
As to dominate Spring but to say it comes
   again.
One day when all flowers bloom in different
   styles,
She stands amid them all and smiles.[6]

(December, 1961)

187

TRANSLATOR'S NOTES

1. Ode to the Plum Blossom: Other implications are possible, but more scholars maintain the plum blossom symbolizes the Chinese Communist Party against the Communist Party of the Soviet Union. The poem was written in December 1961, only one month after the close of the Twenty-Second Congress of the Communist Party of the Soviet Union; during the time, the Chinese Communist Party was attacked by many other communist parties or organizations headed by the Soviet Party whom Mao Zedong deemed as revisionists betraying Marxism and Leninism. At home China's economic situation was rather gloomy then, thus the phrase "icicles hundred-foot long" is not only a factual description of the winter time but also a metaphor alluding to a harsh reality that the Party faced up to.

    This poem had been circulated within the Party for two years before it was published in the 1963 edition of *Poems of Chairman Mao* (People's Literature Press, 1963).

2. Lu You: alias Fang Weng (1125-1210) (Wild Old Man), native of Shanyin (now Shaoxing, Zhejiang), a great poet in the Southern Song Dynasty. Lu You's poems are imbued with ardent patriotism, but the one referred to in Mao Zedong's poem reveals the other side of his style, i. e. graceful and tactful (see his "Ode to the Plum Blossom" on the next page).

188

3. See the poem "Reply to Qin Taixu's 'Ode to the Plum Blossom'" by Su Shi(1037-1101),a poet of the Northern Song Dynasty: "Unaware that it is wind and rain that has sent off spring. "Also see the story "The Jade Bodhisattva" in *Popular Stories of the Capital* ,vol. 10: ". . . while Wang Jinggong(Wang Anshi,1021-1086,a Prime Minister of the Northern Song Dynasty── tr.) saw the flower petals scattered down to the ground by the wind,he thought, so it was the east wind that destoyed spring. "Spring in the poem by Mao stands for the period when socialism was still in bloom;the plum for the Chinese Communist Party.

4. flying snow:the depressing political situation in the world.

5. icicles:hinting at the same as "flying snow".

6. The last two lines are intended to a censure that the Chinese Communist Party was going to usurp the leadership over the International Communist Movement.

附：陆游原词

卜 算 子

bǔ suàn zǐ

詠 梅

yǒng méi

驛外斷橋邊

yì wài duàn qiáo biān

寂寞開無主

jì mò kāi wú zhǔ

已是黃昏獨自愁，

yǐ shì huáng hūn dú zì chóu

更著風和雨。

gèng zhuó fēng hé yǔ

無意苦爭春，

wú yì kǔ zhēng chūn

一任群芳妒。

yī rèn qún fāng dù

零落成泥碾作塵，

líng luò chéng ní niǎn zuò chén

只有香如故。

zhǐ yǒu xiāng rú gù

Lu You's Poem
ODE TO THE PLUM BLOSSOM
to the tune of Song of Divination

By the broken bridge near the post in repose,
She, unseen and forlorn, blazingly blows.
Saddened, she stands alone in the dusk's reign,
Exposed to more attacks from the wind and rain.

With no intention to be the spring's pride,
She ignores the envy from flowers by her side.
When ground to dust and existing no more,
She'll still smell as fragrant as before.

七　律
qī lǜ

冬　雲
dōng yún

雪壓冬雲白絮飛，
xuě yā dōng yún bái xù fēi

萬花紛謝一時稀。
wàn huā fēn xiè yī shí xī

高天滾滾寒流急，
gāo tiān gǔn gǔn hán liú jí

大地微微暖氣吹。
dà dì wēi wēi nuǎn qì chuī

獨有英雄驅虎豹，
dú yǒu yīng xióng qū hǔ bào

更無豪傑怕熊羆。
gèng wú háo jié pà xióng pí

梅花歡喜漫天雪，
méi huā huān xǐ màn tiān xuě

凍死蒼蠅未足奇。
dòng sǐ cāng yíng wèi zú qí

（一九六二年十二月二十六日）

192

WINTER CLOUDS[1]

to the tune of Seven-Character Lü Shi

Catkin-like snow[2] whirls while winter
    clouds hang low,
All of a sudden so many flowers fade or
    die in woe. [3]
In the skies cold waves roll on, swift and
    strong,
On the earth warm breeze gently fans and
    moves along. [4]
Only heroes can drive leopards and tigers[5]
    away,
No brave men would fear wild bears[6] to-
    day.
Plum blossoms[7] like whirling snow scat-
    tered in the sky,
While flies[8] seasonally freeze and tragical-
    ly die.

(December 26, 1962)

TRANSLATOR'S NOTES

1. Winter Cloud: The day on which Mao Zedong wrote the poem was the birthday of Mao at the age of 69.

   This poem was first published in *Poems of Chairman Mao* (People's Literature Press, Peking, 1963).

2. catkin-like snow: The simile is possibly from *New Anecdotes of Social Talk* by Liu Yiqing (403-444) of the Song Dynasty: On a snowing day, Xie An, a scholar, was discussing literature with his nephew and niece; it was snowing harder and Xie An asked with pleasure: "What is the white flying snow like?" Xie Lang, his nephew, answered, "Nearly like salt sprayed in the air." But Xie Daoyun, his niece, retorted, "Better say it is like willow catkins whirling in the wind."

3. Catkin-like snow ... or die in woe: These two lines imply the political situation in the world at the time was depressingly unfavourable to the Chinese Communist Party. Mao thought most of the so-called Marxist Parties in various countries had degenerated into revisionists. Many flowers: many so-called Marxist Parties.

4. On the earth warm breeze gently fans and moves along: (Though the opposition Parties seem powerful,) things gradually take a favourabe turn to the Chinese Communist Party; the brighter future is visible.

194

5. leopards and tigers：referring to imperialists.

6. wild bears：Soviet revisionists；Russian Bears.

7. Plum blossoms：implying the Chinese Communist Party.

8. flies：opportunists who sneaked into the communist ranks.

滿 江 紅
mǎn jiāng hóng

和郭沫若同志
hè guō mò ruò tóng zhì

小小寰球，
xiǎo xiǎo huán qiú

有幾個蒼蠅碰壁。
yǒu jǐ gè cāng yíng pèng bì

嗡嗡叫，
wēng wēng jiào

幾聲淒厲，
jǐ shēng qī lì

幾聲抽泣。
jǐ shēng chōu qì

螞蟻緣槐誇大國，
má yǐ yuán huái kuā dà guó

蚍蜉撼樹談何易。
pí fú hàn shù tán hé yì

正西風落葉下長安，
zhèng xī fēng luò yè xià cháng ān

REPLY TO COMRADE GUO MORUO[1]
to the tune of Riverful Red

Flies,[2]a few, dash themselves against the
    wall
Of this globe small. [3]
Listen! How they hum around the ball,
Shrill with fears
And sob in tears.
Boasting, Ants deem their nest in the lo-
    cust tree a big state,[4]
So funy, mayflies all conspire to shake the
    tree gigantically great. [5]
Now in Chang-an[6] the west wind scatters
    the fallen leaves down
Like whistling arrows flying and gone. [7]

Things are too many indeed
To be done in urgent need.

飛鳴鏑。

fēi míng dí

多少事，

duō shǎo shì

從來急；

cóng lái jí

天地轉，

tiān dì zhuǎn

光陰迫。

guāng yīn pò

一萬年太久，

yī wàn nián tài jiǔ

只爭朝夕。

zhǐ zhēng zhāo xī

四海翻騰雲水怒，

sì hǎi fān téng yún shuǐ nù

五洲震盪風雷激。

wǔ zhōu zhèn dàng fēng léi jī

要掃除一切害人蟲，

yào sǎo chú yī qiè hài rén chóng

全無敵。

quán wú dí

（一九六三年一月九日）

Heaven and earth move around,[8]

Time in greatest demand.

Ten thousand years are too long to delay,

Be sure to seize the night and day.

Four seas[9] rage with clouds and waters in
  anger,

Five continents rock roaring the wind and
  thunder.

To eradicate all pests on this small star,

Mightily invincible we are!

(January 9,1963)

TRANSLATOR'S NOTES

1. On the New Year's Day of 1963, Guo Moruo composed a ci-poem "Feelings on the New Year's Day of 1963——to the tune of Riverful Red. "Guo sent the poem to Mao Zedong and Mao wrote the poem above as a reply.

    This poem was first published in the 1963 edition of *Poems of Chairman Mao* (People's Literature Press, Peking, 1963).

2. flies: here mainly implying what Mao Zedong called Soviet revisionists.

3. this global small: this small globe, the earth. It is small when seen in the boundless space.

4. Ants deem their nest in the locust tree a big state: According to *The Governor of the Southern Tributary State* by Li Gongzuo, a story-teller in the Tang dyansty, a man called Cun Yufen dreamed of a country called Big Locust Tree State and became the son-in-law of the king; he stayed in the state as the governor of the Southern Tributary State for 20 years. One day he was sent back to the human world, awakening to find the state in which he had stayed was nothing but a big ant nest in the locust tree. What had been called the Southern Tributary was only a tiny southern branch of the tree. Mao uses the story to insinuate chauvinism.

5. mayflies all conspire to shake the tree gigantically great: The allusion comes from a poem "Jokingly written to Zhang Ji" (768?-830): "How ridiculous are the mayflies /That conspire to shake the gigantic tree. "The big tree here in the poem is compared to the Chinese Communist Party.

6. Chang-an: the capital of both the Tang and Han dynasties, now Xi-an in Shaanxi Province; here believed to symbolize the head-quarters of hegemonism.

7. whistling arrows flying and gone: The whistling arrow is a weapon invented in the Han Dynasty by Huns, here signifying multiple, even self-contradictory explanations: 1) arrows shot from behind against the Chinese Communist Party (*Journal of the River and Sea*, No. 7, 1964); 2) a signal given by the Chinese Communist Party to attack revisionists; 3) the first attack upon the Chinese Communist Party (*Literature, History and Philosophy*, No. 1, 1964); 4) a gust of cold wind (*Liberation Daily*, October 1, 1964).

8. Heaven and earth move around: The situation in the world is changing.

9. Four seas: all over the world. Ancient Chinese believed that China was surrounded by the four seas; here Four Seas may specifically refer to the Pacific Ocean, the Atlantic Ocean, the Indian Ocean and the Arctic Ocean.

附：郭沫若原词

滿 江 紅
mǎn jiāng hóng

滄海橫流，
cāng hǎi héng liú

方顯出英雄本色。
fāng xiǎn chū yīng xióng běn sè

人六億，
rén liù yì

加強團結，
jiā qiáng tuán jié

堅持原則。
jiān chí yuán zé

天垮下來擎得起，
tiān kuǎ xià lái qíng dé qǐ

世披靡矣扶之直。
shì pī mí yǐ fú zhī zhí

聽雄鷄一唱遍寰中，
tīng xióng jī yī chàng biàn huán zhōng

東方白。
dōng fāng bái

202

Guo Moruo's Poem
to the tune of Riverful Red

It is against the anger of the wild sea
That a hero's mettle is shown to the last degree.
People, six hundred million strong,
If united as one,
With a principle abided by,
Can hold up the falling sky;
If the world goes astray,
They put it in a right way.
Listen! The cock's crow echoes the world at night,
The eastern sky becomes white.

Now out comes the sun,
Melting icebergs anon,
But melting not gold
With the pure quality told.
Four volumes[1] in the people's hand
Serve as a principled stand.
Ridiculous is Jie's dog barking at Yao,[2]
Vanishing into the sea like a clay-made cow.[3]
Behold! The red flags in the wind unfurledly fly,

太陽出，

tài yáng chū

冰山滴；

bīng shān dī

真金在，

zhēn jīn zài

豈銷鑠？

qǐ xiāo shuò

有雄文四卷，

yǒu xióng wén sì juàn

為民立極。

wèi mín lì jí

桀犬吠堯堪笑止，

jié quǎn fèi yáo kān xiào zhǐ

泥牛入海無消息。

ní niú rù hǎi wú xiāo xī

迎東風革命展紅旗，

yíng dōng fēng gé mìng zhǎn hóng qí

乾坤赤。

qián kūn chì

（一九六三年一月一日）

Red is the earth and heaven on high.

(January 1,1963)

Translator's Notes

1. four volumes: referring to *Selected Works of Mao Zedong*, Vol. 1-4, published from 1951 to 1960 in succession.

2. Jie's dog barking at Yao: the tyrant Jie's dog yapping at the sage-king Yao; a pack of hounds barking at a good man. The allusion is from Sima Qian's *The Recordings of History*, V. 83. Jie is said to be an tyrant in the Xia Dynasty (1766 B. C. ?-1122 B. C. ?) while Yao a virtuous king legendarily ruling in the prehistoric period (2255 B. C. ?-2207 B. C. ?). Obviously, Jie's dog could in no way bark at Yao, for there was a time gap of about 440 years between the two ages in which Jie and Yao lived respectively. It is therefore understood that Guo metaphorically uses it to hint at the situation in which some revisionists sided with imperialism to attack the Communist Party of China.

3. clay-made cow: things easy to melt into water; an allusion from "A Monk in Longshan Mountain of Tanzhou" by Shi Daoyuan a scholar in the Song Dynasty: "Dong Shan asked the monk again, 'What reason makes you live in this mountain?' The monk answered, 'I have seen two clay-made cows struggle against each other, vanishing into the sea and never coming back'. " Here Guo refers to what is called reactionaries in the world.

七　律

弔羅榮桓同志

diào luó róng huán tóng zhì

記得當年草上飛，

jì dé dāng nián cǎo shàng fēi

紅軍隊裏每相違。

hóng jūn duì lǐ měi xiāng wéi

長征不是難堪日，

cháng zhēng bú shì nán kān rì

戰錦方為大問題。

zhàn jǐn fāng wéi dà wèn tí

斥鷃每聞欺大鳥，

chì yàn měi wén qī dà niǎo

昆雞長笑老鷹非。

kūn jī cháng xiào lǎo yīng fēi

君今不幸離人世，

jūn jīn bú xìng lí rén shì

國有疑難可問誰？

guó yǒu yí nán kě wèn shuí

（一九六三年十二月）

206

A LAMENT FOR COMRADE LUO RONGHUAN[1]

to the tune of Seven-Character Lü Shï

Remember still those years when you bravely fought,

Of many things in the Red Army we independently thought.[2]

Long March was never unbearable for me and you,

The battle at Jinzhou[3] was a matter of importance true.

It was heard that the quail often sneered at the roc,[4]

From time to time the eagle had to bear the hen's mock.[5]

Alas, now you passed away, our sorrow beyond compare,

Who else can I consult hereafter about the state affair?

(December, 1963)

207

TRANSLATOR'S NOTES

1. Luo Ronghuan: (1902-1963), a native of Hengshan, Hunan Province. After the founding of the People's Republic of China, he was appointed Procurator-General of the Summit Procurate, Director of the General Political Department of the People's Liberation Army, Vice-Chairman of National Defense, member of the Political Bureau of the Central Committee of the Chinese Communist Party.

   This poem was first published in the *People's Daily* (September 9, 1978).

2. we independently thought: The original is obscure in meaning, suggesting possibly 1)often separated from each other; 2)often had different opinions. In 1929, there arose heated dispute over a series of important issues between Mao Zedong and the other Party leaders. Luo was said to have sided with Mao at the time. Later on, Mao Zedong was forced to resign from his leading post and separated from Luo to another place. About four months later in November of the same year, Mao Zedong was restored to his original post. In October 1932, however, Mao was again dismissed from his post by what is called Left opportunists headed by Wang Ming; in Spring 1933, Luo Ronghuan suffered a similar dismissal, and left the First Red Army, thus Mao and Luo separated from each other the second time. It was not until the beginning of the "Long March" that

Mao and Luo were again together.

3. the battle at Jinzhou: In 1948, before the Liaoshen Battle, Mao Zedong gave a directive to the Northwest Field Army that the first target of attack should be Jinzhou, yet, Lin Biao, the commander-in-chief of the Field Army, hesitated to take action, intending to storm Changchun, the capital of Jilin Province first. Luo Ronghuan, the then poiltical commissar of the Northwest Field Army, tried to persuade Lin Biao to follow Mao's strategical plan. Lin finally gave in and the battle for Jinzhou was won. This victory opened up the way for the future victories, therefore Mao deemed the battle at Jinzhou a matter of great importance.

4. the quail often sneered at the roc: an allusion from *Zhuang Zi*: A quail sneers at a roc that flies high and far. The quail and the roc are believed by certain scholars to insinuate the Soviet revisionist leaders and the Chinese Communist Party respectively.

5. the eagle had to bear the hen's mock: an allusion from *Fables of Ivan Andreevich Krylov* (1768—1844): A hen mocks an eagle that happens to fly low. The eagle answers: An eagle indeed sometimes flies low, but a hen can never fly as high as an eagle does. The eagle and the hen are believed to hint at the Chinese Communist Party and the Soviet revisionist leaders respectively.

賀 新 郎

hè xīn láng

讀　　史

dú shǐ

人猿相揖別。

rén yuán xiāng yī bié

只幾個石頭磨過，

zhǐ jǐ gè shí tóu mó guò

小兒時節。

xiǎo ér shí jié

銅鐵爐中翻火焰，

tóng tiě lú zhōng fān huǒ yàn

為問何時猜得，

wèi wèn hé shí cái dé

不過（是）幾千寒熱。

bù guò(shì)jǐ qiān hán rè

人世難逢開口笑，

rén shì nán féng kāi kǒu xiào

上疆場彼此彎弓月。

shàng jiāng chǎng bǐ cǐ wān gōng yuè

流遍了，

liú biàn le

READING HISTORY[1]

to the tune of Congratulating
Bridegroom

Ape and man bowed goodbye to disen-
    gage;[2]
The human beings' childhood stage
Was but a whetstone in the Stone Age.[3]
In stoves were burning the bronze, iron
    and steel,[4]
When did man learn the smelting skill?
Thousands of years passed but hot and
    cold for a while.
In the human world it is hard to find a
    grinning smile,
Killing his own brethren was man's prac-
    tice vile.
Alas, the land so fair
Is soaked in blood everywhere.

郊原血。

jiāo yuán xuè

一篇讀罷頭飛雪，

yī piān dú bà tóu fēi xuě

但記得斑斑點點，

dàn jì dé bān bān diǎn diǎn

幾行陳迹。

jǐ háng chén jī

五帝三皇神聖事，

wǔ dì sān huáng shén shèng shì

騙了無涯過客。

piàn le wú yá guò kè

有多少風流人物？

yǒu duō shǎo fēng liú rén wù

盜跖莊蹻流譽後，

dào zhí zhuāng jué liú yù hòu

更陳王奮起揮黃鉞。

gèng chén wáng fèn qǐ huī huáng yuè

歌未竟，

gē wèi jìng

東方白。

dōng fāng bái

(一九六四年春)

212

My hair now is streaked with snow
When a volume is read through, so
I remember nothing but traces a few
Of the past happenings untrue.
Of Five Emperors[5] and Three Kings[6] the
   recorded holy deeds
Deceived countless people, now and then,
   of all breeds.
How many genuine heroes were there in
   history after all?
Only, Zi the bandit[7] and Jue the rebel[8]
Who should now deserve the fame without
   a fall
And Chen the slaves' king[9] who once
   wielded
The battle ax of bronze as a call.
Now in the east breaks the day
Before I finish this epic lay.

(Spring, 1964)

TRANSLATOR'S NOTES

1. Reading History: This poem is a reflection upon the major phases of human development.

    The poem was first published in the *People's Daily* (September 9, 1978).

2. Ape and man bowed goodbye to disengage: Ape and man are believed by Charles Robert Darwin(1809-82)to be of the same ancester; or in another word, Darwin derives the human race from a hairy quadrumanous animal belonging to the great anthropoid group, and related to the progenitors of the orangutan, chimpanzee and gorilla. The evolution of man from ape has gone through a period of about three million years.

3. the Stone Age: the initial development of human beings spanning a period of about two or three million years during which mankind's productive tools were chiefly made of stone.

4. In stoves were burning the bronze, iron and steel: referring to the ages of bronze and iron.

5. Five Emperors: five legendary rulers in ancient China: Huang Di (2698? B. C. -2598? B. C.), Zhuan Xu (2514? B. C. -2436? B. C.), Di Ku (2436? B. C. -2366? B. C.), Yao (2357? B. C. -2257? B. C.), Shun (2255? B. C. -2207? B. C.).

6. Three Kings: 1) Fu Xi, Shen Nong, Huang Di; 2) the King of Heaven, the King of earth, the King of Man.

7. Zi the bandit: the leader of the slave rebels at the end of the Spring and Autumn Period (770B. C. -476B. C.). See the chapter "Zi the Bandit" in *Zhunag Zi*: "Zi the bandit... with his nine thousand followers, rode roughshod throughout the country and outraged the dukes and nobles"; and the chapter "Be Careful" in *Xun Zi*: "Zi the bandit enjoys a name as shining as the sun and moon, and as lasting as the reputation of Shun and Yu. "

8. Jue the rebel: the leader of the slave rebellion that took place in the State of Chu in the Warring States Period (475B. C. -221B. C.)

9. Chen the slaves' king: Chen Sheng (?-208B. C.), a native of Yangcheng (now Dengfeng of Henan Province), the leader of the slave uprisings that broke out at the end of the Qin Dynasty (221B. C. -207B. C.).

水調歌頭
shuǐ diào gē tóu

重上井岡山
chóng shàng jǐng gāng shān

久有凌雲志，
jiǔ yǒu líng yún zhì

重上井岡山。
chóng shàng jǐng gāng shān

千里來尋故地，
qiān lǐ lái xún gù dì

舊貌變新顏。
jiù mào biàn xīn yán

到處鶯歌燕舞，
dào chù yīng gē yàn wǔ

更有潺潺流水，
gèng yǒu chán chán liú shuǐ

高路入雲端。
gāo lù rù yún duān

過了黃洋界，
guò le huáng yáng jiè

216

REASCENDING JINGGANG MOUNTAIN[1]

to the tune of Prelude to
Water Melody

With a long-cherished clouds-reaching
    ideal,[2]
I again visit Jinggang Mountain with zeal.
Covering a thousand miles to view the old
    land,
I see the former scene become newly
    grand.
Everywhere swallows dance, orioles sing,
And streams splash and ring,
A high way[3] mounts to the cloud's wing.
The boundary of Huangyangjie[4] is passed
    once,
No other passes deserve a glance.[5]

Behold! In this human world

險處不須看。
xiǎn chù bù xū kàn

風雷動，
fēng léi dòng

旌旗奮，
jīng qí fèn

是人寰。
shì rén huán

三十八年過去，
sān shí bā nián guò qù

彈指一揮間。
tán zhǐ yī huī jiān

可上九天攬月，
kě shàng jiǔ tiān lǎn yuè

可下五洋捉鱉，
kě xià wǔ yáng zhuō biē

談笑凱歌還。
tán xiào kǎi gē huán

世上無難事，
shì shàng wú nán shì

只要肯登攀。
zhǐ yào kěn dēng pān

（一九六五年五月）

Wind and thunder[6] are heard to roar,

Flags and banners gaudily soar.

Thirty-eight years are past,

So quickly as if you snapped a finger fast. [7]

Up in the Ninth Heaven[8] we can pluck the-
moon,

Down in the Five Oceans[9] we may seize turtles soon,

In triumph we return with laughters and
songs boon.

In this world nothing is hard to do,

Try scaling the heights, success attend
you!

(May, 1965)

219

TRANSLATOR'S NOTES

1. Reascending Jinggang Mountain: Mao Zedong and his men went to Jinggang Mountains in October 1927. Thirty-eight years later on May 22 to 29, 1965, Mao revisited the place while he made an inspection tour of the regions south as well as north of the Yangzi River. See notes to "Jinggang Mountain——to the tune of Moon over West River" and "Jinggang Mountain——to the tune of Charm of Maiden Niannu".

   This poem was first published in *Poetry* (January 1976).

2. clouds-reaching ideal: a pun implying 1) lofty aspirations, great ambition; 2) a wish for a revisit to Jinggang Mountain which towers into the sky. *History of Later Han Dynasty*, XXVIII: "Feng Yan often claimed himself to be one who possesses a cloud-reaching ideal."

3. A high way: a way built in the winter of 1960, leading to Jinggang Mountain from Ningganglong of Jiangxi Province.

4. Huangyangjie: See the note to "Jinggang Mountain——to the tune of Moon over West River".

5. The boundary... deserve a glance: metaphor, implying if one has gone through the sort of struggle waged in the Jinggang Mountain, no other kind of difficulty deserves a mention.

6. Wind and thunder: metaphor, the revolution waged by the proletariat.

7. as if you snapped a finger fast: as if you snapped a finger very quickly; a phrase of buddhism, meaning a flash of time.

8. the Ninth Heaven: the highest heaven.

9. Five Oceans: the Pacific Ocean, the Atlantic Ocean, the Indian Ocean, the Arctic Ocean and the Antarctic Ocean; the last one should be the Antarctic Continent and may be regarded here as a kind of poetic licence.

念 奴 嬌

niàn nú jiāo

鳥兒問答

niǎo ér wèn dá

鯤鵬展翅，九萬里，

kūn péng zhǎn chì jiǔ wàn lǐ

翻動扶搖羊角。

fān dòng fú yáo yáng jiǎo

背負青天朝下看，

bèi fù qīng tiān cháo xià kàn

都是人間城郭。

dōu shì rén jiān chéng guō

炮火連天，

pào huǒ lián tiān

彈痕遍地，

dàn hén biàn dì

嚇倒蓬間雀。

xià dǎo péng jiān què

怎麼得了，

zěn me dé liǎo

A DIALOGUE BETWEEN
TWO BIRDS[1]

*to the tune of Charm
of Maiden Niannu*

Spreading his wings, the roc[2]
Soars ninety thousand li to shock
The atmosphere into storms[3] that unlock.
Flying beneath the blue sky, looking down,
He finds the human world covered by the
    city and town.
The heaven-licking gunfire is heard,
Shells everywhere render the earth laired,
And a sparrow in the bush gets scared:[4]
"Oh, how terrible here to stay,
I must at once fly away!"

"Tell me where your destination lies?"
The sparrow replies:

哎呀我要飛躍。
āi yā wǒ yào fēi yuè

借問君去何方，
jiè wèn jūn qù hé fāng
雀兒答道：
què ér dá dào
有仙山瓊閣。
yǒu xiān shān qióng gé
不見前年秋月朗，
bú jiàn qián nián qiū yuè lǎng
訂了三家條約。
dìng le sān jiā tiáo yuē
還有吃的，
hái yǒu chī de
土豆燒熟了，
tǔ dòu shāo shú le
再加牛肉。
zài jiā niú ròu
不須放屁，
bù xū fàng pì
試看天地翻覆。
shì kàn tiān dì dì fān fù

（一九六五年秋）

224

" To a fairies ' hill where jaded palaces
   rise. [5]

The autumn moon shone brighter two years
   ago

When three sides signed a pact, [6]don't you
   know?

There are also things to chew:

Potatoes cooked well,

With beef added, too. " [7]

No passing wind, you bird,

Look, the heaven and the earth are upside
   down transferred. [8]

(Autmun, 1965)

TRANSLATOR'S NOTES

1. A Dialogue Between Two Birds: In 1960's, there among the communists throughout the world arose the great polemics over some essential principles concerning Marxism and Leninism. Both the Communist Party of China and the Communist Party of Soviet Union plunged themselves into the debate and were ideologically and diametrically opposed to each other. The roc in the poem stands for the Communist Party of China while the sparrow in the bush the Soviet revisionists.

    This poem was first published in *Poetry* (January 1976).

2. the roc: one of the two birds. See notes to "From Tingzhou to Changsha——to the tune of Butterflies Love Flowers" and "A Lament for Comrade Luo Ronghuan".

3. storms: storms of revolution in the world.

4. a sparrow in the bush gets scared: revisionists in general; particularly referring to those who believe that a spark of dispute might give rise to a world war and even finally destroy the whole mankind.

5. a fairies' hill where jaded palaces rise: alluding to a theory of rendering the world into one without troops, arms and wars.

6. three sides signed a pact: referring to the convention on prohibition of nuclear experiment within atmosphere, outerspace and under the sea signed by Great Britain, the United States

226

and Soviet Union in Moscow in July and August, 1963. Mao Zedong regarded the convention as a political fraud intended to maintain the monopoly of nuclear powers within several countries while depriving the rest of the countries of the right to experiment with nuclear weapons.

7. Potatoes cooked well, /With beef added, too: On April 1, 1964, in a factory of Budapest, Hungary, Nikita khrushchev generalized what he called communism as a need for a good dish of potatoes well cooked with beef.

8. the heaven and the earth are upside down: On January 30, 1962, at an extended meeting of the Central Committee of the Chinese Communist Party held in Peking, Mao Zedong said: "From now on, the period of about fifty years or one hundred years will be a great age, in which the social systems of the world will see a thorough change and the heaven and the earth will be upside down; it will be an era that will come to pale any other periods in history. "

副 編

Part Two

送縱宇一郎東行
sòng zòng yǔ yī láng dōng xíng

雲開衡嶽積陰止，
yún kāi héng yuè jī yīn zhǐ

天馬鳳凰春樹裏。
tiān mǎ fèng huáng chūn shù lǐ

年少峥嶸屈賈才，
nián shào zhēng róng qū jiǎ cái

山川奇氣曾鍾此。
shān chuān qí qì céng zhōng cǐ

君行吾為發浩歌，
jūn xíng wú wèi fā hào gē

鯤鵬擊浪從兹始。
kūn péng jī làng cóng zī shǐ

洞庭湘水漲連天，
dòng tíng xiāng shuǐ zhǎng lián tiān

艟艨巨艦直東指。
chōng méng jù jiàn zhí dōng zhǐ

SEEING JUU ICHIRO[1] OFF TO JAPAN

to the tune of Seven-Character
Ancient Odes

Over Hengyue Mountain[2] dark clouds dis-
    perse and cold current flees,
Heavenly Horse and Phoenix Mountains[3]
    are seen covered with spring trees.
Here are bred outstanding scholars like Qu
    Yuan[4] and Jia Yi[5], gifted and young,
The spirit and essence of mountains and
    rivers all here throng. [6]
For your leave-taking I now chant a hearty
    song,
The roc[7] cleaves through the waves right
    from now on.
The waters of Dongting Lake[8] and Xiang
    River[9] rise into the sky,
The great steamship will soon in the sea

無端散出一天愁，

wú duān sàn chū yī tiān chóu

幸被東風吹萬里。

xìng bèi dōng fēng chuī wàn lǐ

丈夫何事足縈懷，

zhàng fū hé shì zú yíng huái

要將宇宙看稊米。

yào jiāng yǔ zhòu kàn tí mǐ

滄海橫流安足慮，

cāng hǎi héng liú ān zú lù

世事紛紜何足理。

shì shì fēn yún hé zú lǐ

管却自家身與心，

guǎn què zì jiā shēn yǔ xīn

胸中日月常新美。

xiōng zhōng rì yuè cháng xīn měi

名世于今五百年，

míng shì yú jīn wǔ bǎi nián

諸公碌碌皆餘子。

zhū gōng lù lù jiē yú zǐ

平浪宮前友誼多，

píng làng gōng qián yǒu yì duō

崇明對馬衣帶水。

chóng míng duì mǎ yī dài shuǐ

eastward ply.

Anyhow the sky is full of grief your heart
cannot allay,

Thanks to the east wind that scatters the
grief ten thousand miles away.

There is nothing to worry about for a true
man, I advise,

You'd better regard the universe as tiny as
a grain of rice.

The adverse current in the sea[10] is but a
mere trifle at all,

Secular affairs in disorder should not your
attention call.

Take care of the cultivation of your own
body and mind, and do

Keep the sun and moon in your heart beautiful and new.

Just five hundred years past since the birth
of the last great man,[11]

All the other figures in powers now are of
a mediocre clan.

In front of the Pinglang House[12] is shown

東瀛濯劍有書還，
dōng yíng zhuó jiàn yǒu shū huán

我返自崖君去矣。
wǒ fǎn zì yá jūn qù yǐ

（一九一八年春）

sincere friendship,

The Chongming[13] and Tsushima Islands[14]
are separated only by a water strip

When you are in Japan from you we'll be
eager to hear,

But let's say goodbye to you right now and
here.

(Spring,1918)

TRANSLATOR'S NOTES

1. Jūu Ichiro: alias of Luo Zhanglong (1896-?), a native of Liu-
yang County, Hunan Province, Mao Zedong's classmate in
No. 1 Associated Middle School of Changsha in 1915. He was
one of the initiators of the organization of the Chinese Communist Party in Peking. But in January 1931, he was expelled
from the Party for what was called the Right opportunist
splitting activities.

2. Hengyue Mountain: Hengshan, with 72 peaks, situated in the
middle of Hunan.

3. Heavenly Horse and Phoenix Mountains: three mountains belonging to the Yuelu Mountain Ranges: the Big Heavenly
Horse Mountain, the Small Heavenly Horse Mountain and the

Phoenix Mountain.

4. Qu Yuan: also called Qu Ping (340B. C. -278B. C.), a great Chinese poet and statesman in the period of the Warring States. Being out of favour with the King of Chu and finding no way to realize his political ambition, he finally committed suicide by drowning himself in the Mieluo River, leaving behind some poems such as "Li Sao" (A Lament), usually regarded by many Chinese men of letters as the greatest poetic efforts in classical Chinese literature.

5. Jia Yi (200 B. C. -168 B. C.): a talented man of letters and a statesman in the Western Han Dynasty. He rose to fame when he was eighteen years old.

6. The line implies the place is noted for an abundance of men of talents.

7. the roc: See notes to "March from Tingzhou to Changsha", "A Dialogue between the Two Birds" and "A Lament for Comrade Luo Ronghuan".

8. Dongting Lake: See note 6 to "Reply to a Friend——to the tune of Seven-Character Lü Shi".

9. Xiang River: See note 3 to "Changsha——to the tune of Spring Beaming in Garden".

10. The adverse current in the sea: the great political chaos.

11. Just five hundred years past since the last great man: See the chapter "Gongsun Chou" in *The Book of Mencius*, 4. 13: "It is

236

a rule that a true Imperial sovereign should arise in the course of five hundred years, and that during that time there should be men illustrious in their generation. From the commencement of the Zhou Dynasty till now, more than 700 years have elapsed. Judging numerically, the date is past. Examining the character of the present time, we might expect the rise of such individuals in it. But Heaven does not yet wish that the empire should enjoy tranquillity and good order. If it wished this, who is there besides me to bring it about? How should I be otherwise than dissatisfied?"

12. Pinglang House: a palace of Taoism, located in Changsha.

13. Chongming: the name of an island, situated in the north of Shanghai, the entrance of the Yangzi River to the East Sea.

14. Tsushima Islands: the name of islands of Japan.

西江月

xī jiāng yuè

秋收起义

qiū shōu qǐ yì

军叫工农革命，

jūn jiào gōng nóng gé mìng

旗号镰刀斧头。

qí hào lián dāo fǔ tóu

匡庐一带不停留，

kuàng lú yī dài bù tíng liú

要向潇湘直进。

yào xiàng xiāo xiāng zhí jìn

地主重重压迫，

dì zhǔ chóng chóng yā pò

农民个个同仇。

nóng mín gè gè tóng chóu

秋收时节暮云愁，

qiū shōu shí jié mù yún chóu

霹雳一声暴动。

pī lì yī shēng bào dòng

（一九二七年）

238

THE AUTUMN HARVEST UPRISINGS
to the tune of Moon over West River

The insurgent army of workers and peasants is our name,
The emblem of our banners is the sickle
and ax in a frame.
In the district of Kuanglu we shall not
stay,
But press straight on to Hunan without delay.

Landlords' oppression is so heavey to bear
That all the peasants hate it and roundly
swear.
Just in autumn harvest season when evening clouds pout,
Like a thunderbolt from the sky the rebellion breaks out.

(1927)

六言詩

liù yán shī

給彭德懷同志

gěi péng dé huái tóng zhì

山高路遠坑深，

shān gāo lù yuǎn kēng shēn

大軍縱橫馳奔。

dà jūn zòng héng chí bēn

誰敢橫刀立馬？

shuí gǎn héng dāo lì mǎ

唯我彭大將軍。

wéi wǒ péng dà jiāng jūn

（一九三五年十月）

TO COMRADE PENG DEHUAI[1]

to the tune of
Six-Character Poetry

Mountains high, roads long, and valleys
    deep,
Mighty armies through Northern Shaanxi
    sweep.
Who dare with sword drawn sharp stop
    his steed?[2]
Only Peng, our great general, indeed!

(October, 1935)

TRANSLATOR'S NOTES

1. Peng Dehuai: (1898-1974), a native of Xiangtan, Hunan Province; commander of the Fifth Red Army, Vice-Chairman of the Military Commission of the Central Committee of the Communist Party of China, Vice-Premier of the State Council, Minister of National Defense. At Lushan Meeting in 1959, Peng Dehuai was unjustly criticised for what was called Right opportunism; later on he was more seriously persecuted by the "gang of four"; he died in disgrace on November 29, 1974. See note 1 to "Ascent of Lushan Mountain".

    This poem was first published in *Newspapers of Comrades-in-Arms* (August 1, 1947) sponsored by the armies of Hebei-Shandong-Henan, and republished in *Literature and Art of People's Liberation Army* (April, 1957) and in the 1986 edition of *Selected Poems of Mao Zedong* (People's Literature Press, Peking, 1986).

2. Who dare with sword drawn sharp stop his steed: Who dare stop his steed with sword drawn sharp. On October 19, 1935, the Central Committee of the Chinese Communist Party and Anti-Japanese Vanguard Troops under the command of Peng Dehuai reached the Town of Wuqi, Shaanxi Province, when five Kuomintang cavalry regiments were in hot pursuit. In order to prevent the cavalry regiments from entering the revolutionary base area in northern Shaanxi, the advance troops led

242

by Peng Dehuai fought fiercely and wiped out one cavalry regiment at Damaoliang near the Town of Wuqi. Because this was the first victory won by the Red Army after it reached northern Shaanxi, Mao Zedong wrote a six-character-line poem (the only one in this form in Mao's collection of poems) in praise of Peng Dehuai's martial feat. Peng, on receiving the poem, modestly changed the last line into "Only our heroic red armies indeed", and sent the revised version to Mao Zedong.

临 江 仙
lín jiāng xiān

给丁玲同志
gěi dīng líng tóng zhì

壁上红旗飘落照，
bì shàng hóng qí piāo luò zhào

西风漫捲孤城。
xī fēng màn juǎn gū chéng

保安人物一时新。
bǎo ān rén wù yī shí xīn

洞中开宴会，
dòng zhōng kāi yàn huì

招待出牢人。
zhāo dài chū láo rén

纤笔一枝谁与似？
xiān bǐ yī zhī shuí yǔ sì

三千毛瑟精兵。
sān qiān máo sè jīng bīng

阵图开向陇山东。
zhèn tú kāi xiàng lǒng shān dōng

TO COMRADE DING LING[1]
to the tune of Immortal at Riverside

The red flags over the wall[2] fluttering in the
    setting sun,
The west wind caressing the separate
    town,
Now in Bao'an[3] county new heroes throng.
An entertaining banquet is offered to hail
A heroine who was just released from jail.

What can be compared to her slender pen?
With Mauser-rifles[4] three thousand picked
    men.
Beyond north of Longshan[5] our war plan is
    under way,
A literary lady yesterday,
Now a general in battle array.

(1936)

245

昨天文小姐，

zuó tiān wén xiǎo jiě

今日武將軍。

jīn rì wǔ jiāng jūn

（一九三六年）

TRANSLATOR'S NOTES

1. Ding Ling:also called Jiang Yiwen(1904-1986),a native of Hunan,communist writer. On May 14,1933,Ding Ling was kidnapped by the Kuomintang special agents in Shanghai and was put under house arrest for three years. On September 18, 1936,she made a successful escape with the help of the Chinese Communist Party. In October of the same year,she went to Xi-an in disguise and from there she went to the Bao'an County, northern Shaanxi. Mao Zedong, Zhou Enlai, Zhang Wentian and Bo Gu gave her a warm welcome. When asked what she was going to do there in the base area,she answered "To be an Red Army soldier". On November 22,1936,the first literary circle in the liberated area—China's Literature and Art Association—was founded. Ding Ling was elected Chairman of the body. On December 30,1936,Ding Ling received the poem sent by Mao Zedong by telegram when she was in the Red Army pressing on to southern China. Then at the beginning of 1937,Ding Ling came to Yenan,and Mao Zedong rewrote the poem with a writing brush, giving it again to Ding.

This poem was first published in *New Observation* (July, 1980).

2. the wall:the city wall of the Baoan County.

3. Bao'an:a town situated in the northwest of Shaanxi,the head-

247

quarters of the Chinese Communist Party then.

4. Mauser-rifles: powerful repeating rifles invented by Paul Mauser (1838-1914), a German inventor. Sun Yat-sen said on August 24, 1922, in his "A Talk with the Newspaper": "It is often said that a pen is mightier than three thousand Mauser-rifles. "

5. Longshan: a mountain situated in the northwest of the Long County, Shaanxi Province.

6. our war plan is under way: On December 12, 1936, Xi-an Incident took place; the main force of the Red Army moved southward to Xi-an with an intention to fight against the Kuomintang troops, in cooperation with Northeastern Army and Northwestern Army when Chiang Kai-shek was detained by his own subordinates Zhang Xueliang and Yang Hucheng in Xi-an. Ding Ling, at the that time, was in the southward Red Army.

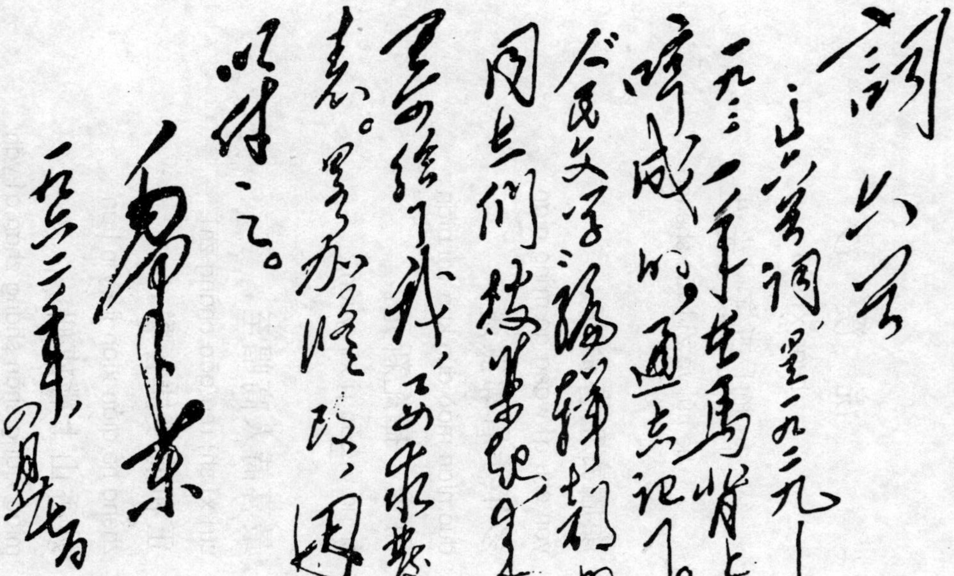
词六首
这六首词，是一九二九——一九三一年在马背上哼成的，通忘记了。人民文学编辑部的同志们搜集起来，寄给了我，要求发表，略加改正，因以付之。
毛泽东
一九六二年，四月廿七日

浣 溪 沙
huàn xī shā

和柳[亞子]先生
hè liǔ [yà zǐ] xiān shēng

颜斶齊王各命前，
yán chù qí wáng gè mìng qián

多年矛盾廓無邊，
duō nián máo dùn kuò wú biān

而今一掃紀新元。
ér jīn yī sǎo jì xīn yuán

最喜詩人高唱至，
zuì xǐ shī rén gāo chàng zhì

正和前綫捷音聯，
zhèng hé qián xiàn jié yīn lián

妙香山上戰旗妍。
miào xiāng shān shàng zhàn qí yán

(一九五〇年十一月)

250

REPLY TO MR. LIU YAZI[1]

to the tune of
Silk-Washing Stream

Yan Chu and King of Qi ordered each other
to come on,[2]
The contradictions between them are deep
for years long,[3]
Now everything changes into a new age.[4]

What is the most pleasant is our poet's
loud song
Echoing the victory news from the front,
the battle stage.
Look! How bright are the war banners on
Mount Myohyang.[5]

(November,1950)

TRANSLATOR'S NOTES

1. Reply to Mr. Liu Yazi: On October 4 and 5, 1950, after watching the opera *Pigeon of Peace*, in Huai Ren Hall of Zhong Nan Hai, Peking, Mr. Liu Yazi wrote a poem to the tune of Silk-Washing Stream. The next month, Mao Zedong replied Liu's poem to the same tune.

   This poem was first published in the 1986 edition of *Selected Poems of Mao Zedong* (People's Literature Press, 1986).

2. Yan Chu and King of Qi ordered each other to come on: an allusion from *Records of the Warring States*: When the king of Qi received Yan Chu, his subject, he said, "Come up to me, Chu." Yan Chu also said, "Come up to me, my king." The King of Qi was displeased. The other subjects said to the king, "Your Majesty is the king of all men; Chu is only your subject. Is it appropriate for Chu to ask Your Majesty to come up to him when Your Majesty demands he come up to you?" To this, Chu answered, "I come up to his Majesty only for flattering the power of king, but his Majesty comes up to me for his intention to approach worthy subjects. It would be better for His Majesty to approach worthy subjects than for Chu to flatter the power of king." The King of Qi changed his colours angrily, questioning: "Who is nobler, king or king's subjects?" Chu answered: "King is not noble, but king's subjects are."

252

Here Mao Zedong compares the King of Qi to Chiang Kai-shek and Yan Chu to Liu Yazi: Chiang was not willing to be courteous to the wise or condescending to the scholarly while Liu was upright and never stooping to flattery.

3. The contradictions between them are deep for years: Early in 1926, Liu Yazi openly repudiated Chiang Kai-shek as a brand-new warlord; they had been at feud with each other for many years ever since.

4. Now everything changes into a new age: Everything changes for the better after the founding of the People's Republic of China.

5. Mount Myohyang: Myohyang-Sanjulgi a mountain situated in the northwest of Korea; referring to the Korean War.

七　律

qī　lǜ

和周世钊同志

hè zhōu shì zhāo tóng zhì

春江浩荡暂徘徊，

chūn jiāng hào dàng zàn pái huái

又踏層峰望眼開。

yòu tà céng fēng wàng yǎn kāi

風起綠洲吹浪去，

fēng qǐ lǜ zhōu chuī làng qù

雨從青野上山來。

yǔ cóng qīng yě shàng shān lái

尊前談笑人依舊，

zūn qián tán xiào rén yī jiù

域外鷄蟲事可哀。

yù wài jī chóng shì kě āi

莫歎韶華容易逝，

mò tàn sháo huá róng yì shì

卅年仍到赫曦臺。

sà nián réng dào hè xī tái

（一九五五年）

254

TO ZHOU SHIZHAO[1]

to the tune of
Seven-Character Lü Shi

By the mighty spring river[2] I linger erewhile
with you,
Then we ascend the jagged peaks to com-
mand a wider view.
The wind from the green islet[3] blows the
waves without a stop,
The rain over the emerald field now moist-
ens the mountain top.
At the feast we chat as before, our former
selves restored,
Pitiful are those chicken-and-worm affairs[4]
abroad.
Don't lament that time and youth too
quickly fly,
Thirty years later today[5] we again gather at
Hexitai. [6]

(1955)

255

TRANSLATOR'S NOTES

1. Zhou Shizhao: See Mao's "Reply to a Friend —— to the tune of Seven-Character Lü Shi".

    In a letter to Zhou Shizhao, dated October 4, 1955, Mao Zedong says, "I am interested in your poetic efforts and now I have replied to one of your Lü Shi poems; please don't stint your criticism." Zhou Shizhao was then the president of No. 1 Middle School of Hunan Province, and his poem was entitled "Ascending Yuelu Mountain with Chairman Mao".

    This poem was first published in the 1983 edition of *Selected Letters of Mao Zedong* (People's Press, Peking, 1983).

2. spring river: referring to the Xiang River. See note 1 to "Changsha".

3. the green islet: the Orange Island in the Xiang River. See note 2 to "Changsha".

4. those chicken-and-worm affairs: alluding to Du Fu's poem "Binding Chicken for Worms" in which Du Fu uses chicken-and-worm relationship as a metaphor to hint at those who are preying upon one another; worms are eaten by chickens and in turn chickens are eaten by human beings. Lu Xun once wrote a poem "An Elegy on Fan Ainong" (July 22, 1912), using the same metaphor to satirize the snobbish person He Jizhong, Fan Ainong's colleague, for his preying upon people in lower positions. One is apt to be lured into thinking of Hamlet's mad

256

words in his dialogue with King Claudius where the beggar (Hamlet) eats fish, fish eats worms, worms eat king (and Polonius), king (and Polonius) eats maggots, and finally maggots eat beggar (*Hamlet*, IV. iii. 16-31). So the organic world in a sense exsists in a way of mutual production and destruction as all living things exist in a great chain of being. But here some scholars suggest that the metaphor is intended by Mao Zedong to insinuate the power strife within the Soviet revisionist leaders.

5. Thirty years later today: In Autumn of 1925, Mao Zedong left Shaoshan, his native place, for Guangzhou, via Changsha where he made a visit to Yuelu Mountain and places near the mountain; he also wrote a poem "Changsha——to the tune of Spring Beaming in Garden". Now in 1955, just thirty years since then, he again came to the same spot.

6. Hexitai: a platform on top of the Yuelu Mountain, built in 1528.

念 奴 嬌
niàn nú jiāo

井 冈 山
jǐng gāng shān

参天萬木，
cān tiān wàn mù

千百里，
qiān bǎi lǐ

飛上南天奇嶽。
fēi shàng nán tiān qí yuè

故地重來何所見，
gù dì chóng lái hé suǒ jiàn

多了樓臺亭閣。
duō le lóu tái tíng gé

五井碑前，
wǔ jǐng bēi qián

黄洋界上，
huáng yáng jiè shàng

車子飛如躍。
chē zǐ fēi rú yuè

江山如畫，
jiāng shān rú huà

JINGGANG MOUNTAIN[1]

to the tune of Charm
of Maiden Niannu

Amid millions of towering trees in age
Stretching hundreds of li, I fly
Onto the top of a mountain so strange
    in the southern sky.
Revisiting the old land what I have in view
Are many pavillions and towers new.
There Huangyangjie[2] still lies,
And the Five-Well Tablets[3] rise,
Past them my car quickly flies.
Mountains and rivers are picture-like[4] and
    sublime,
But they are said to be a green sea in an-
    cient time.

As if with a snap of fingers

古代曾云海綠。

gǔ dài céng yún hǎi lǜ

彈指三十八年，

tán zhǐ sān shí bā nián

人間變了，

rén jiān biàn le

似天淵翻覆。

sì tiān yuān fān fù

猶記當年烽火裏，

yóu jì dāng nián fēng huǒ lǐ

九死一生如昨。

jiǔ sǐ yī shēng rú zuó

獨有豪情，

duó yǒu háo qíng

天際懸明月，

tiān jì xuán míng yuè

風雷磅礴。

fēng léi páng bó

一聲鷄唱，

yī shēng jī chàng

萬怪煙消雲落。

wàn guài yān xiāo yún luò

（一九六五年五月）

Past are thirty-eight years;[5]

Oh , how the human world changes its
    gown

As heaven and sea are upside down![6]

Remember still the war fires neigh

And narrow escapes from death on our way

Happen as if it were yesterday.

Only, our sentiments and aspirations so
    high

Are like the bright moon hanging in the
    distant sky

Like the wind and thunder majestically
    sweeping by.

Hear! The cock now crows aloud,[7]

All monsters disappear like vanished smoke
    and cloud.

(May,1965)

TRANSLATOR'S NOTES

1. Jinggang Mountain: See note 1 to "Jinggang Mountain —— to the tune of Moon over West River". For the background information of the poem, see note 1 to "Reascending Jinggang Mountain——to the tune of Prelude to Water Melody".

   This poem was first published in the 1986 edition of *Selected Poems of Mao Zedong* (People's Literature Press, 1986).

2. Huangyangjie: See note 2 to "Jinggang Mountain —— to the tune of Moon over West River".

3. the Five-Well Tablets: indicaters of five places in the Jinggang Mountain area, i. e. the Large Well, the Small Well, the Up Well, the Middle Well, and the Down Well.

4. Mountains and rivers are picture-like: an allusion from the poem "Reflections at the Red Cliff upon the Ancient Heroes—— to the tune of Charm of Maiden Niannu "by Su Shi (Su Dongpo, 1036-1101), a great poet and scholar in the Northern Song Dynasty: "Mountains and rivers are picture-like, /Reminiscent of the heroes that thronged the fleeting age. "It also reminds us of Mao Zedong's own line in "Snow—— to the tune of Spring Beaming in Garden": "With so much beauty is the land endowed, /So many heroes thus in homage bowed. "

5. Past are thirty-eight years: See note 1 to "Jinggang Moun-

262

tain——to the tune of Moon over West River".

6. Heaven and earth are upside down: Great changes have taken place in the human world.

7. The cock now crows aloud: See Mao's "Reply to Mr. Liu Yazi——to the tune of Silk-Washing Stream": "At a crow of the cock the dark world is suddenly exposed to light."

Appendices

關於詩的一封信

克家同志和各位同志：

惠書早已收到，遲覆為歉！遵囑將記得起來的舊體詩詞，連同你們寄來的八首，一共十八首，抄寄如另紙，請加審處。

這些東西，我歷來不願意正式發表，因為是舊體，怕謬種流傳，貽誤青年；再則詩味不多，沒有什麼特色。既然你們以為可以刊載，又可為已經傳抄的幾首改正錯字，那末，就照你們的意見辦吧。

《詩刊》出版，很好，祝它成長發展。詩當然應以新詩為主體，舊詩可以寫一些，但是不宜在青年中提倡，因為這種體裁束縛思想，又不易學。這些話僅供你們參考。

同志的敬禮！

毛澤東

一九五七年一月十二日

A LETTER ABOUT POETRY

Comrade Kejia and others,

Sorry not to have replied sooner to your letter
which I have received in early time! Here are enclosed,
at your request, 18 traditional-styled poems (including
the eight which you sent to me) copied from my memory
on separate sheets of paper; please examine them and do
what you deem fitting about them.

I have been reluctant to publish these stuffs with a
fear that, being in traditional style, if inappropriately
diseminated, they might do young people harm, and,
what is more, they are not so poetic and unique. Since
you think that they can be published, and that, in addition, the publication helps a correction of copying errors
in a few poems already in circulation, you may act according to your own opinion.

The publication of *Poetry* is a good thing; I wish
the magazine would grow and develop. As for poetry
creation, the main stream certainly should be free verse
in vernacular; poetry in traditional style can be tried to a
limited degree, but it is improper to encourage the at-

tempt among the young, because it is a bondage of thought as well as a difficult thing to learn. These words are only for your reference.

With comradely greetings!

Mao Zedong
January 12, 1957

給胡喬木同志的信

喬木同志：

　　詩兩首，請你送給郭沫若同志一閱，看有什麼毛病沒有？加以筆削，是為至要。主題雖好，詩意無多，只有幾句較好一些的，例如"雲橫九派浮黃鶴"之類。詩難，不易寫，經歷者如魚飲水，冷暖自知，不足為外人道也。

毛澤東

九月七日

A LETTER TO COMRADE HU QIAOMU

Comrade Qiaomu,

Enclosed here are two poems; please send them to comrade Guo Moruo for a check so that all possible faults in them be duly corrected; it is essentially important. The subject matter is good, but it is not poetic enough, with only a few lines such as "Clouds sail over the nine streams with the Yellow Crane in flight" sounding fairly good. Poetry composition is a difficult job; he who has experienced it knows the hot and cold just as fish drink water. I really have little about it to reveal to the outsiders.

Mao Zedong
September 7,1959

271

給陳毅同志談詩的一封信

陳毅同志：

　　你叫我改詩，我不能改。因我對五言律，從來沒有學習過，也没有發表過一首五言律。你的大作，大氣磅礴。只是在字面上（形式上）感覺于律詩稍有未合。因律詩要講平仄，不講平仄，即非律詩。我看你于此道，同我一樣，還未入門。我偶爾寫過幾首七律，沒有一首是我自己滿意的。如同你會寫自由詩一樣，我則對于長短句的詞學稍懂一點。劍英善七律，董老善五律，你要學律詩，可向他們請教。

西　行

　　萬里西行急，乘風御太空。
　　不因鵬翼展，那得鳥途通。
　　海釀千鍾酒，山栽萬仞葱。
　　風雷驅大地，是處有親朋。

只給你改了一首，還很不滿意，其餘不能改了。

　　又詩要用形象思維，不能如散文那樣直說，所以比、興兩法是不能不用的。賦也可以用，如杜甫之《北征》，可謂"敷陳其事而直言之也"，然其中亦有比、興。"比者以彼物比此物也"，"興者，先言他物以引起所詠之詞也"。韓愈

A LETTER TO COMRADE CHEN YI ABOUT POETRY

Comrade Chen Yi,

You asked me to polish your poems, but I am unable to because I have never learnt how to compose five-character-line poetry, neither have I published any in that form. Your masterpiece is of power and range except that it does not sound metrically quite a Lü Shi[1], at least on the surface. Lü Shi, as is known, is bound up with tonal patterns; without which a poem is not to be called Lü Shi. It seems you, like me, are not disciplined enough in this respect. I have written a few seven-character-line Lü Shi accidentally, but none of them satisfies me. Just as you are good at writing free verse, I know a little Ci[2] of long-and-short lines. Jianying[3] is good at seven-character-line Lü Shi, and old comrade Dong[4] at five-character-line Lü Shi. If you want to learn these two forms well, you may ask them for advice.

Journeying Westward

For ten thousand li westward I speed,
Crossing the space I ride the wind like a steed.

以文為詩；有些人說他完全不知詩，則未免太過，如《山石》，《衡嶽》，《八月十五酬張功曹》之類，還是可以的。據此可以知為詩之不易。宋人多數不懂詩是要用形象思維的，一反唐人規律，所以味同嚼蠟。以上隨便談來，都是一些古典。要作今詩，則要用形象思維方法，反映階級斗爭與生產斗爭，古典絕不能要。但用白話寫詩，幾十年來，迄無成功。民歌中倒是有一些好的。將來趨勢，很可能從民歌中吸引養料和形式，發展成為一套吸引廣大讀者的新體詩歌。又李白只有很少幾首律詩，李賀除有很少幾首五言律外，七言律他一首也不寫。李賀詩很值得一讀，不知你有興趣否？

祝好！

毛　澤　東

一九六五年七月二十一日

> *But for the roc's wings that spread and display,*
> *How could man traverse the bird's distant way.*
> *The sea below ferments a thousand cups of wine,*
> *And mountains like onions roar into heaven nine.*
> *The wind and thunder sweep the great earth,*
> *And there we find good friends of great worth.*

I have polished only one of your poems as above, being not satisfied with the result; I am afraid I cannot continue polishing the rest.

By the way, poetry calls for images to convey ideas and should not communicate in a straight-forward way as in prose; thus a poet must resort to the means of *Bi* (similes and metaphors) and *Xing* (assocations of images). The technique of *Fu* (direct narration) may be also employed as in Du Fu (Tu Fu)'s "Northern Journey", which may be said to "narrate in a straightforward way", but even here one can find that both *Bi* and *Xing* are used. "*Bi* means to compare one object to another"; "*Xing* means to mention something else to lead up to what a poet really has in mind". Han Yu[5] writes poetry by using prose techniques, therefore he is criticised as knowing nothing about poetry; but the criticism is going too far, for, some of his poems such as "Rocks", "Hengyue Mountains" and "To Mr. Zhang the Prefectural Offical on the Fifteenth Day of the Eighth

Moon" are acceptable, after all. This fully shows that poetry writing is not an easy job. Most poets of the Song Dynasty, being at odds with the tradition of Tang Poetry, do not understand that poetry conveys ideas through images; the result being that they write very dry poems. These random remarks above all refer to classical poetry. To write modern poetry, we must use images to convey ideas in order to reflect class struggle and the struggle for production. Classicism must be excluded. It is a pity that for scores of years, attempts at poetry in the vernacular have never been successful. Nevertheless, some folk-songs are quite good; it is very likely that the future trend of poetry is to draw nourishment and adopt new forms from the folk-song and develop a new type of poetry which will appeal to the general reading public. By the way, Li Bai(Li Po)has only a few Lü Shi to his name; Li He(Li Ho)never wrote seven-character-line Lü Shi except several five-character-line ones. Li He is well worth reading. I wonder if you are interested in him. With best wishes,

Mao Zedong
July 21,1965

TRANSLATOR'S NOTES

276

1. Lü Shi: a traditional form of classical Chinese poetry, with strict tonal patterns and rhyme schemes. It has eight lines with five or seven characters in each; extremely popular in the Tang Dynasty.
2. Ci: a verse form originating in the Tang Dynasty. It is sung to tunes each of which prescribes a fixed number of lines of a standardized varying length.
3. Jianying: Ye Jianying, the late Vice-Chairman of the Central Military Committee of the Chinese Communist Party.
4. old comrade Dong: Dong Biwu, a communist statsman, Mao's colleague.
5. Han Yu(768—824): a noted prose writer and poet of the Tang Dynasty.

索引　　INDEX

284

286

　290

291

300

譯 注 者 簡 介

辜正坤,北京大學英語系文學博士,碩士研究生導師,北大文學與翻譯研究學會會長兼莎士比亞研究中心主任,國際詩歌研究會理事,深圳大學外文系客座教授。歷獲北京大學科研成果一等獎,北京市高校中青年哲學社會科學優秀獎,全國首屆中青年翻譯理論優秀獎,全國圖書金鑰匙獎等。主要著、譯、編著作有《莎士比亞研究》(英文專著,巴黎莎士比亞書店8c 公司,1993),《中國歷代名詩三百首選注》(北京出版社,1993),《外國名詩三百首選注》(北京出版社,1993),《辜正坤抒情詩精華》(香港新世紀出版社,1993),《元散曲英譯》(合譯)(香港新世紀出版社,1986),《世界名詩鑑賞詞典》(北大出版社,1990),《世界詩歌鑑賞大典》(臺灣地球出版社,再版本,上下卷,1992),《第三世紀》(人民出版社,1990),《林肯文集》(上卷,三聯書店,1993),《英國浪漫派散文精華》(作家出版社,1989),《美國文學精華》(主校譯,川師大出版,1985),《中國二十世紀純抒情詩精華》(作家出版社,1991),《張愛玲散文精粹》(作家出版社,1992)等。用中外文在國內外發表論文100余篇。現于北大英語系。曾為研究生講授過莎士比亞,詩歌,翻譯理論與實踐和古希臘羅馬文學史等課程,兼《世界文學與翻譯研究》雜志主編。通英語、法語、古希臘語、古拉丁語及世界語等。1993年應邀任聯合國教科文組織總部(巴黎)翻譯。

About the Translator and Annotator

Gu Zhengkun, Ph. D. of Department of English of Peking University, president of Peking University Literature and Translation Society, director of Shakespeare Centre, member of the Governing Council of International Society for Poetry, guest professor of Foreign Languages Department of Shenzhen University. He is also the winner of many honours and awards such as the First Prize for Academic Achievement awarded by the authority of Peking University (1991), Social Siences Award for the Middle-aged College Teachers offered by the Educational Bureau of the City of Peking (1992), the National Translation Theory Prize (1989) and the National Gold Key Book Award (1991). He is the author of *Studies in Shakespeare* (*in English*, 1993), *Appreciation of* 300 *Masterpieces in World Poetry* (1993), *Appreciation of* 300 *Masterpieces in Classical Chinese Poetry* (1993), *Selected Poems of Gu Zhengkun* (1993); translator of *Highlights of the Yuan Dynasty Lyrics* (*into English*, 1986), *The Third Century* (1990), *A Collection of Abraham Lincoln's Speeches and Letters* (*Vol.* 1) (1993); editor-in-chief of *A Companion to Masterpieces in World Poetry* (1990), *Highlights of English Romantic Prose* (1989), *Highlights of American Literature* (1985), *Highights of* 20*th Century Chinese Lyrics* (1990), *Highlights of Zhang Ailin's Prose* (1992). He has published more than 100 articles at home and abroad either in English or in Chinese. He has been teaching Peking University postgratuate students Shakespeare, Poetry, Translation Theory and Practice, History of Greek and Roman Literature. He is currently the editor-in-chief of *Studies in World Literature and Translation*. He knows well English, French, Old Greek, Latin and Esperanto. In 1993, he was invited by UNESCO (Paris) as a translator.